# Hedging Currency Exposures

# HEDGING CURRENCY EXPOSURES

Brian Coyle

## Glenlake Publishing Company, Ltd
Chicago • London • New Delhi

### AMACOM
## American Management Association

New York • Atlanta • Boston • Chicago • Kansas City • San Francisco • Washington, D.C.
Brussels • Mexico City • Tokyo • Toronto

This book is available at a special
discount when ordered in bulk quantities.
For information contact Special Sales Department,
AMACOM, an imprint of AMA Publications, a division of
American Management Association,
1601 Broadway, New York, NY 10019

This publication is designed to provide accurate and authoritative
information in regard to the subject matter covered. It is sold
with the understanding that the publisher is not engaged in
rendering legal,accounting, or other professional service. If
legal advice or other expert advice is required, the services of
a competent professional person should be sought.

ISBN: 0-8144-0616-5

Printing number

10 9 8 7 6 5 4 3 2 1

# Contents

# Currency Risk

Currency risk arises from the potential consequences of an adverse movement in foreign exchange rates. There are three types of exposure to currency risk: transaction, translation and economic.

# Transaction Exposures

A transaction exposure starts with a commitment (or intention) to receive income in foreign currency or to make a foreign currency payment at some future point. Foreign currency income would be converted into another currency, typically, domestic currency. Foreign currency payments would be paid for by purchasing the amount of currency required, typically, in exchange for domestic currency. The risk from the exposure is that cash income in the domestic currency will turn out lower than expected, or that cash payments in the domestic currency will turn out higher than expected.

- Losses on adverse exchange rate movements could have a significant impact on net profits for the company concerned.
- Exposures could arise for a short time, or could last over a longer period.
- For a company that regularly buys or sells abroad, short-term exposures will arise continually, and the company always will have some currency exposure.

Currency risk is two-way in the sense that exchange rates could move favorably rather than adversely during the period of exposure, resulting in a gain or unexpected profit.

*Example 1*

A company sells goods abroad at a price of $120,000 with the customer given six months' credit. The company intends to convert its dollar income into sterling. At the time of the transaction, the exchange rate was £1 = $1.50, and the company expected eventually to receive £80,000 (120,000 ÷ 1.50).

*Analysis*

From the time of the transaction to the customer payment six months later, the company has a dollar income exposure of $120,000 and is at risk to a fall in the value of the dollar against sterling. In six months' time, if the dollar exchange rate is, for example, £1 = $1.60, the company's sterling income from its dollar receipts will be just £75,000, or £5,000 less than expected. The loss from the adverse exchange rate movement would be £5,000.

Suppose that the cost to the company of selling the goods was £77,000 so that its expected profit was £3,000. A change in the sterling/dollar rate to $1.60 would more than wipe out this expected profit, and leave the company with a £2,000 loss.

The exchange rate during the period of exposure could move in the company's favor, with the dollar strengthening in value. If the exchange rate after six months is £1 = $1.40 for example, the company would receive £85,714 (120,000 ÷ 1.40) from the transaction, and gain £5,714 from the favorable dollar movement (compared to the expected income of £80,000 at the exchange rate of $1.80 when the transaction was originally made).

*Example 2*

A company buys goods from Hong Kong for HK$120,000, and must pay for them in three months. The rate of exchange is $1 = HK$20, and the company plans to buy the Hong Kong dollars at this rate (120,000 ÷ 20 = $6,000) in three months' time to pay its supplier.

*Analysis*

During the period between making the purchase and paying the supplier, the company has a Hong Kong dollar exposure of HK$120,000. It is at risk to an increase in the value of the Hong Kong dollar during the exposure period. If the exchange rate after three months were $1 = HK$18, the company would have to spend $6,666 to buy the required dollars. This would be $666 more than expected, and would represent a loss to the company on the exchange rate movement. The company's costs would be higher than planned, and its profit margins therefore would fall.

If the Hong Kong dollar fell in value during the period of the currency exposure, the purchase price of the Hong Kong dollars in US dollars also would fall and there would be a profit from the favorable exchange rate movement.

# Translation Exposures

Translation exposures occur only because of the financial reporting requirements to produce consolidated accounts for a group of companies, and to translate the financial position of foreign subsidiaries into the currency of the parent company. Investments in foreign subsidiaries must be translated into an equivalent amount of the currency of the group's parent.

- If the value of a foreign subsidiary's currency has fallen the group will have to report a foreign exchange loss on its investment.
- In addition, translating the subsidiary's profits for the year into the parent company's currency also will be affected by the exchange rate movement.

Translation exposures affect reported profits and balance sheet values, but, unlike transaction exposures, they do not involve cash gains or losses, unless a cash dividend is declared by a foreign subsidiary (when a transaction exposure arises for the dividend receivable by the parent company). For this reason, companies could regard translation exposures as far less significant and worrying than transaction exposures.

*Example*
A UK company has two subsidiaries, one in Germany and one in the US. Financial results for these companies are as follows:

| | German subsidiary | US subsidiary |
| --- | --- | --- |
| Year 1 profits | €378,000 | $480,000 |
| Balance sheet, end of Year 1 | € | $ |
| Assets | 2,457,000 | 3,840,000 |
| Bank loans | -491,400 | -960,000 |
| Net assets (= equity investment) | 1,965,600 | 2,880,000 |
| Year 2 profits | 312,000 | 480,000 |
| Exchange rates | | |
| End of Year 1 | £1 = €1.50 | £1 = $1.50 |
| End of Year 2 | £1 = €1.40 | £1 = $1.60 |

To prepare consolidated accounts for the group, the parent company translates the profits and investments in its foreign subsidiaries at the year-end rate of exchange.

There were no dividend payments by either foreign subsidiary for Year 2.

*Analysis*
Translation exposures arise in two ways.

*Profits.* The profits of both subsidiaries were the same in Year 2 as in Year 1, at €378,000 and $480,000 respectively. These are translated into sterling and added to the group's consolidated profits for the year, using the year-end exchange rate.

|  | German subsidiary £ |  | US subsidiary £ |
|---|---|---|---|
| Year 1 profits | (378,000 ÷ 1.5) 252,000 | (480,000 ÷ 1.5) | 320,000 |
| Year 2 profits | (378,000 ÷ 1.4) 270,000 | (480,000 ÷ 1.6) | 300,000 |
| Change in reported profits | +18,000 |  | -20,000 |

Reported profits in the group's financial accounts will vary with movements in the exchange rate, even when the subsidiary's profitability in its own currency is constant. For a public company conscious of a need to report buoyant profits to its shareholders, such gains or losses can be significant.

*Net investment value.* The value of the group's reported investment in its foreign subsidiaries is also affected by exchange rate movements.

### Investment in Subsidiary at End of Year 1

|  | German subsidiary (Translated into sterling) |  |  |
|---|---|---|---|
|  |  | At Year 1 rate (÷ 1.60) | At Year 2 rate (÷ 1.40) |
|  | € | £ | £ |
| Assets | 1,433,600 | 896,000 | 1,024,000 |
| Bank loans | -286,720 | -179,200 | -204,800 |
| Net assets (= equity investment) | 1,146,880 | 716,800 | 819,200 |
| Change (increase in value) |  |  | + 102,400 |

| | | US subsidiary (Translated into sterling) | |
|---|---|---|---|
| | | At Year 1 rate (÷ 1.5) | At Year 2 rate (÷ 1.6) |
| | $ | £ | £ |
| Assets | 3,840,000 | 2,560,000 | 2,400,000 |
| Bank loans | -960,000 | -640,000 | -600,000 |
| Net assets (= equity investment) | 2,880,000 | 1,920,000 | 1,800,000 |
| Change (loss in value) | | | -120,000 |

Changes in the value of the net investment from favorable or adverse exchange rate movements are gains or losses on foreign exchange, which affect the group's reported balance sheet position. The exchange gains or losses on translation of asset values are offset to some extent by the translation of bank loans and other liabilities. In this example, the group had gains on its euro assets and losses on its dollar assets that were partially offset by losses on its US euro loans and gains on its dollar loans. The translation exposure in each currency is the net amount of assets minus liabilities.

# Economic Exposures

Economic exposures arise when the trading position of a business is at risk to adverse movements in exchange rates. These exposures can be either short term or long term.

*Direct economic exposures* are a company's expected future receipts and payments in foreign currency, where specific transactions have not yet been made. For example, a Norwegian oil company, selling its North Sea output in dollars, will know that it can expect future dollar income from its oil sales. It has continuing economic exposures because of its dollar income, and is at risk from a decline in the dollar's value.

*Indirect economic exposures* are the long-term risks to a business from adverse economic developments in the country in which it is based, resulting in exchange rate movements that benefit foreign competitors.

### Example 1

A Spanish company competes with a US company and a Brazilian company, for markets in the European Union and the US. The costs per unit are €10 to the Spanish company, $11 to the US company and BRR22 to the Brazilian company. The selling price per unit of product is €15 in Europe and $16.50 in the US.

Exchange rates are €1 = $1.10, €1 = BRR2.20 and $1 = BRR2

### Analysis

At these costs, exchange rates and selling prices, all three companies are equally competitive in the European and US markets.

Suppose, however, that exchange rates changed as follows

€1 = $1.50
€1 = BRR3.00
$1 = BRR2.00

The euro has strengthened against both the dollar and the Brazilian real, but the relative value of the Brazilian real and the dollar against each other is unchanged.

The consequences for the Spanish company would be devastating. In the US market, where the product is sold for $16.50, the Spanish company would now earn revenue of just €11 per unit, and because the cost of sale is €10, sales to the US would be barely profitable.

In the European market, the Spanish company will come under threat from low-cost producers in the US and Brazil. The cost of selling each unit is €10 to the Spanish company, whereas the equivalent cost of production to the US and Brazilian competitors is now about €7.33 ($11 or BRR22). Both could reduce their market price in Europe and still make a profit. By dropping the price below €10, they would most probably force the Spanish company out of business.

*Example 2*
During the early-to-mid 1980s, the dollar strengthened in value against most other currencies. As a result, German and Dutch beer producers were able to increase their sales to the US, winning about 5% of the market. When the dollar's value weakened in 1987, falling to its 1980 level against the deutschemark and the guilder, imported beer prices increased substantially and US beer producers were able to recover lost market share.

*Analysis*
Both the European and US beer producers had economic exposure to the exchange rate for the dollar against European currencies. A strong dollar improved European competitiveness and a weak dollar improved the price competitiveness of US producers.

Beer producers, both in Europe and the US, will have difficulty preparing a long-term market strategy so long as the dollar exchange rate is volatile and their economic exposures to the value of the dollar are not hedged.

# Assessing the Currency Risk

By monitoring currency exposures, management can assess the significance of the risk and make decisions about what measures if any should be taken. The factors to consider are

- *Size of the exposure* (relative to the size of the company's cash flows and profits). For example, an exposure to dollar payments of $250,000 over a given period of time will be more significant for a German company that is expecting profits of just €50,000 than for a company expecting profits of €500,000.

- *Nature of the exposure.* Transaction exposures, because of their potential consequences for cash flows, normally will be regarded by management as more significant than translation exposures and indirect economic exposures.
- *Certainty of the exposure.* Decisions by management to deal with an exposure often will depend on the degree of certainty in the estimates of foreign currency receipts and payments, and whether an estimated future exposure actually will materialize.
- *Probable direction of exchange rate movements.* There are occasions when the movement in an exchange rate is more likely to be up than down (or vice versa) in the period of the exposure. For example, in a badly performing economy the country's currency is likely to weaken over a period of time. A foreign/ multinational company with regular expenditures in that currency therefore might decide that its exposure is small. On the other hand, a foreign/multinational company exposed to earning regular income in that currency might decide that its exposure is significant and that risk-management action is definitely required.

Having identified a currency risk and quantified the exposure, it is relatively simple to determine how serious the risk might be. This can be done by making an assumption about exchange rate volatility, i.e. about the possible change in the exchange rate over the period of the exposure.

*Example*

A UK company expects to pay $150,000 and ¥10,000,000 for two purchase contracts. Both amounts will be paid in three months. The current exchange rates are £1 = $1.50 and £1 = ¥100, and so a cost of £100,000 is expected for each purchase.

During the three-month period, suppose sterling might weaken against the dollar by 10% to £1 = $1.3500, and by a smaller amount against the yen to £1 = ¥98.

*Analysis*

The potential loss can be quantified as

| Exposure | Current exchange rate | Expected cost | Possible exchange rate | Possible cost | Risk of loss |
|---|---|---|---|---|---|
| | | £ | | £ | £ |
| $150,000 | 1.50 | 100,000 | 1.3500 | 111,111 | 11,111 |
| ¥10,000,000 | 100 | 100,000 | 98 | 102,041 | 2,041 |

# 2

# The Hedging Decision

Measures to reduce or eliminate an exposure to risk are referred to as hedging. The terms hedging an exposure and hedging a risk are used interchangeably.

Hedging action could have one of the following outcomes

- complete avoidance of the exposure
- partial avoidance of the exposure
- elimination of the exposure by fixing in advance an effective exchange rate for a future foreign currency transaction.

## Should Exposures be Hedged?

Deciding whether or not to hedge currency exposures will depend on

- how significant the potential risk is considered to be, and
- the company's attitude to currency risk.

For most financial institutions, hedging currency risks is essential. Non-bank companies have different opinions regarding hedging. Those that favor hedging all exposures argue that a failure to hedge is a decision to take a position in the market and so incur risk. In contrast, those that favor selective hedging argue that the costs and effort of hedging are justified only when an adverse movement in exchange rates can be foreseen, making such an action profitable.

A number of non-bank companies allow their dealing rooms to

speculate in foreign currencies, and so do not confine their trading to hedging operations.

# Attitude to Risk

A company's attitude to risk can be risk neutral, risk averse or risk seeking.

A *risk neutral* attitude accepts risks as and when they arise, and doesn't view hedging action as necessary. Such an attitude might be justified if

- the exposures are small and insignificant
- gains and losses from exchange rate movements will roughly balance each other, thus making hedging action unnecessary.

A *risk averse* attitude is normal for most companies with significant transaction exposures. Although gains and losses on exchange rate movements might balance out over the longer term, the short-term consequences of an adverse exchange rate movement (for one or more currencies) could be serious for both cash flows and profitability. Risk averse management therefore could seek to hedge all significant exposures.

A *risk-seeking attitude* is based on the view that exchange rates will move in the company's favor and that currency exposures will result in gains rather than losses. A company taking this view welcomes the exposures and will seek where possible, and within reason, to increase and exploit them.

# How Much Exposure to Hedge?

A large company should have a clear policy for hedging its currency exposures so that its finance or treasury staff know what is expected of them and what they must not do.

**Hedging Action: the Choices**

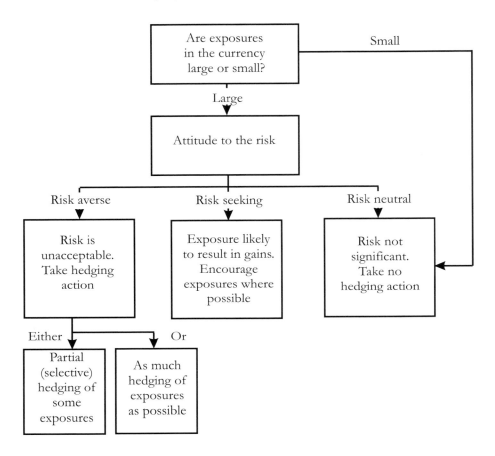

The amount of cover a company wants its treasury department to transact should be specified. For example, company policy might stipulate

- 100% cover for exposures arising in the next six months
- 75-100% cover for exposures expected in the next six to 12 months
- 50-75% cover for exposures expected in one to two years
- 25-50% cover for exposures expected in the next two to four years

- 0-25% cover for exposures expected in four or more years.

Management should be kept aware of the size of the potential currency risks facing the company and limits placed on permissible currency exposures. For example, a management might specify that exposures in dollar income must not exceed $5 million in any 12-month period. In addition, there should be a clear policy on whether to allow speculative trading for profit.

Choosing not to hedge exposures should be a conscious decision taken in the belief that either the exposure is insignificant or there is a good prospect of favorable exchange rate movements or exchange rate stability. It should not be a choice made out of ignorance or disregard for the risks from exposure.

*Imposing a Time Limit on Exposures*

If a company accepts that its currency exposures are unavoidable or not worth hedging, it can still restrict the size of its exposures by putting a time limit on them.

- In tendering for a contract abroad, a company could put a time limit on the bid it submits. For example, a tender for a contract in dollars made on July 1 could be priced at $2 million with the offer remaining open for three months until September 30.
- If a company issues price lists in foreign currency, they can have a limited life span of perhaps three or six months, after which they will be replaced.

# Hedging Policies

Policies to hedge or to avoid currency risks can take several forms, including

- shifting the risk to others

- improving productivity and reducing costs
- leading and lagging payments
- structural hedging
- hedging with treasury instruments.

### Shifting the Risk

In foreign trade, either the supplier or the customer often will trade in domestic currency; thus the immediate or tangible foreign currency exposure falls on just one of them. In reality, both supplier and customer face a currency risk.

A company could try to insist on paying for imported goods in its own domestic currency. If foreign suppliers agree to payment in the customer's domestic currency, the immediate currency transaction risk will then fall on them. The hidden risk to the customer, however, is that if the domestic currency increases in value against the supplier's currency, it might end up paying more than rival companies in other countries. If the customer's domestic currency falls in value, however, foreign suppliers simply will raise their selling prices. For example, suppose an electronics company buys components from Japan, and pays $2 per unit with the exchange rate being $1 = ¥100. The Japanese supplier will be receiving the equivalent of ¥200 per unit. If the rate changes to $1 = ¥120, the supplier could continue to charge $2 and benefit from an effective price increase to ¥240. On the other hand, if the rate changes to $1 = ¥80, the supplier could increase his price to $2.50 to ensure that he still receives ¥200 per unit.

An exporter similarly can insist on payment for its exported goods in his domestic currency. The currency transaction risk falls on the customers abroad, but the exporter has economic exposure to the risk of his domestic currency strengthening in value against other currencies. Shifting the immediate currency risk to a foreign customer does not remove the risk, it merely masks it.

A strategy of shifting risk on to suppliers or customers might be acceptable for one-off transactions, but is incompatible with the concepts of

- suppliers as partners in the value chain, and
- customer care that maintains the business relationship.

*Productivity and Reducing Costs*

The management of a well-run business will seek to minimise costs without jeopardising the quality of its products or services. Productivity improvements are a well-established method of reducing costs, and enhancing a firm's competitiveness against rival companies, including foreign competition. Many companies focus their energies on lowering their unit costs of production to ensure effective competition in foreign markets, however much their domestic currency/currency of expenditures strengthens relative to their competitors' currencies.

*Example*
A US company exports goods to Germany priced in dollars. The exchange rate at the start of the year is €1 = $0.6500. During the year the euro strengthens to €1 = $0.5850. The weaker euro hurts the US exporter because exports priced in dollars will now cost German customers more.

*Analysis*
If the US company can reduce its costs and prices by 10% to 90% (0.5850/0.6500) of what they were before, it could offset the effect of the adverse exchange rate movement. A product that used to sell for $100 could be reduced to $90, and German customers would pay the same as before – €153.85.

*Leading and Lagging Payments*

When a company is concerned about an adverse movement in exchange rates, it might protect itself against the risk by either

- making foreign currency payments before the payment is due, or
- by delaying foreign currency payments if possible until after the due date.

For example, if a company has to pay a supplier $480,000 in six months' time, and expects the dollar to strengthen in value against sterling, it might decide to pay now rather than later. If the current exchange rate is £1 = $1.60, the payment will cost £300,000. If in six months' time the exchange rate is £1 = $1.50, the payment would cost £320,000. The company would have saved £20,000 by paying early.

Similarly, suppose that a UK company expects to pay €180,000 to a French supplier in three months' time, but expects the value of the euro to decline sharply. If the exchange rate after three months is €1 = £0.60, the payment would cost £108,000. By delaying payment, if the euro falls to €1 = £0.50, the lagged payment would cost only £90,000 and the company would have saved £18,000.

Shifting the risk to customers or suppliers, improving productivity and reducing costs can only partly hedge currency risks. Other hedging policies usually will be needed also. A task of financial management is to identify the most suitable policy, combining structural hedging and hedging with treasury instruments.

# 3

# Transaction-based Structural Hedging

A fundamental rule of foreign currency risk management is to minimize exposures where possible by netting (matching) exposures that occur in opposite directions. This is called structural hedging and can be achieved in two ways: transaction-based structural hedging and strategic structural hedging. Transaction-based structural hedging, also known as offset hedging, involves

- setting off income against expenditure in the same currency, or
- setting off assets against liabilities in the same currency.

# Foreign Currency Income

Cash inflows in one currency can be matched against cash payments to be made at the same time and in the same currency. Currency risk is eliminated to the extent that matching takes place.

*Example 1*
A German company will receive $150,000 in late March, and pay out $80,000 at the same time. Exposure to the currency risk can be reduced to $70,000 by matching the payment against the income, and using some of the dollar income to make the dollar payment. If another dollar payment of $30,000 is due in early April, this too could be offset against the income, leaving a net exposure of $40,000 that it could hedge in another way. (The company could hold its dollars in an interest-earning dollar bank account until the payment is made.)

**Offset hedging: Foreign Currency Income**

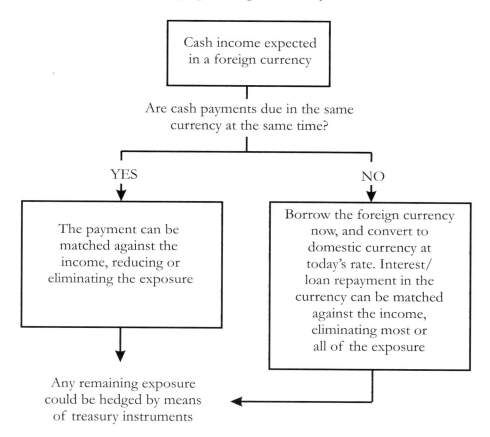

*Example 2*

A French company forecasts that in July it should receive $5 million from overseas sales and pay $3 million to overseas suppliers and agents. This forecast is based on estimates of future sales and expenditures, none of which have yet occurred.

The company expects an exposure to a net income of $2 million in July, but this is only an estimate. The actual exposure could be higher or lower. Even so, management normally would use offset hedging where possible to try to make dollar payments out of dollar income, and hedge an estimated net exposure of $2 million by other methods.

*Borrowing to Create a Structural Hedge*

When a company expects future income in a foreign currency, and wishes to hedge the risk of a fall in its value over the period of the exposure, it can create a structural hedge by

- borrowing in the currency, with the loan's maturity matched to the date that the currency income eventually will be received, and
- converting the borrowed currency into domestic currency at the current spot rate.

This fixes the rate of exchange for the eventual currency income. Interest on the foreign currency loan and repayment of the loan principal would be paid out of the currency income when it is earned (at the maturity of the loan), thereby creating a currency payment to match the receipt.

*Example*

A UK company will receive $249,000 in six months' time. Interest on dollar loans is 7.5% per annum, and the company borrows $240,000 at this rate for six months. The dollars are converted immediately into sterling, and if the spot exchange rate is £1 = $1.50, it will receive £160,000 (240,000 ÷ 1.50).

After six months, the loan principal of $240,000 will be repaid (plus interest of $9,000 for six months) out of the dollar receipts of $249,000.

By arranging this structural hedge, the company has fixed the exchange rate for its dollar income. However, the company has the benefit of £160,000 for six months. The funds could be invested at a UK interest rate, and the effective exchange rate that the company has secured will depend on the interest rate obtainable. If the £160,000 could be invested for six months at 7.5% per annum (the same as the dollar interest rate) to earn interest of £6,000, the effective exchange rate from the structural hedge and loan transaction would be

Dollar/Conversion value into sterling
= £166,000/$249,000 which is
= £1 = $1.50

# Foreign Currency Payments

A similar approach can be adopted to hedge exposures where cash payments are expected to exceed income in the same currency. Again, the currency risk is eliminated to the extent that matching takes place.

**Offset hedging: Foreign Currency Payments**

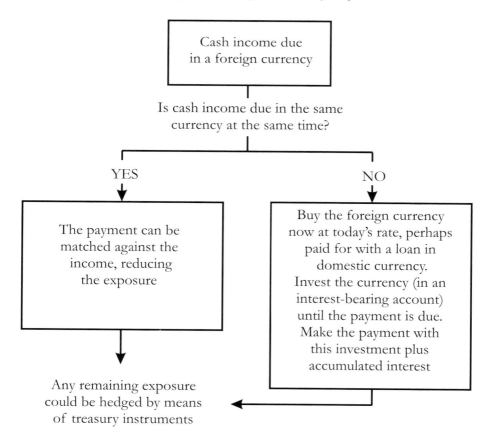

*Example*

A US company must make a payment of €100,600 in three months' time to a supplier in the Netherlands. It expects to receive €40,000 at the same time from a customer.

Today's spot rate for the euro against dollars is €1 = $0.60. The interest rate available on dollar deposits is 6% p.a. and on the euro interest is 4%.

*Analysis*

To hedge partially its exposure to the euro payment, the company can offset the income of €40,000 and use this money towards the payment. This leaves a net exposure of €60,600 (100,600 - 40,000).

This remaining exposure can be hedged by purchasing €60,000 now, and putting these on deposit at 4% p.a. (1% per quarter) to earn €60,600 after three months (60,000 x 1.01). The cost of buying the euros now at €1 = $0.60 would be $36,000. This money could have been kept in dollars and invested at 6% p.a. for three months. The company's dollar cost of buying the euros, including interest foregone, would be $36,540 (36,000 x 1.015). The effective cost to the company of the €60,600 therefore is $36,540 that means the company has locked in an exchange rate now of €1 = $0.6030 (36,540/60,600) for the future payment of €60,600.

# Foreign Currency Accounts

Foreign currency bank accounts can help a company match its cash income and cash payments more easily, enhancing the efficiency of structural hedging as a form of exposure management. This is because the timing of any matching does not have to be exact. Currency income can be kept in the account to be matched against imminent payments, and an overdraft facility can be negotiated for payments occurring shortly before receipts of income in the currency.

A foreign currency account in any major traded currency can be opened with most major retail banks. A company should be aware of the bank's charges for the service, and its planned use of the account ought to be sufficient to justify the cost.

Substantial cash balances on a foreign currency account should be avoided, however, (unless the currency is thought to be increasing in value) because foreign currency cash balances create another currency exposure. For example, $500,000 on deposit with a bank is a foreign currency asset for a Spanish company, and unless it is holding the money to make a future dollar payment as a structural hedge, the company will be at risk to a fall in the dollar against the euro. Similarly, large overdrafts on a currency account will create an exposure, and therefore should be avoided, unless the currency is expected to fall in value or the overdraft is for a structural hedge and will be paid off out of future income in that currency.

# Foreign Currency Assets and Foreign Currency Liabilities

When a company has a foreign subsidiary, the currency exposure can be reduced by borrowing in the same currency. Assets and liabilities in the currency can be matched and netted off against one another.

*Example*
A UK company has a subsidiary in the US with assets valued at $630,000.

The UK company or the US subsidiary could borrow in dollars, to reduce or eliminate this translation exposure. For example, the US subsidiary might be financed partly by a dollar loan of $200,000. If the parent company, or another company in the group, borrowed $430,000, the dollar assets could be matched exactly against the dollar liabilities, and the translation exposure would be eliminated.

Any change in the sterling/dollar exchange rate would create a matching gain or loss on translation of the group's assets and liabilities into sterling when the consolidated accounts are prepared.

For example, if the exchange rate is £1 = $1.50, the dollar assets and liabilities, translated into sterling for the group accounts, would be

|  | £ |
| --- | --- |
| Assets ($630,000 ÷ 1.50) | 420,000 |
| Loans ($630,000 ÷ 1.50) | 420,000 |
| Net assets | 0 |

If the exchange rate changes to £1 = $1.575 when the group accounts are next prepared, the position will be as follows:

|  | Current value in sterling | Previous translated value | Gain or loss on translation |
| --- | --- | --- | --- |
|  | £ | £ | £ |
| Assets ($630,000 ÷ 1.575) | 400,000 | 420,000 | -20,000 |
| Loans ($630,000 ÷ 1.575) | 400,000 | 420,000 | +20,000 |
| Net assets | 0 | 0 | 0 |

The fall in the sterling value of the dollar assets is a loss on translation, and the fall in the sterling value of the dollar loans is a gain. The loss and gain offset each other exactly. In the same way, if the exchange rate were to move in the other direction, with the dollar gaining value against sterling, there would be an increase in the sterling value of both the dollar assets and the dollar liabilities. The gain on translation of the asset values would be offset by a loss on the increased value of the loans.

Some transaction exposures also would occur in this example from dividends, management charges and royalties paid by the US subsidiary to the UK parent, and from payments of interest on dollar loans. To some extent, these exposures can be reduced by transaction-based structural hedging, matching receipts of dividends, etc. in dollars to interest payments on the dollar loans.

# Cross Matching of Currencies

Cross matching of currencies is a method of hedging based on the principle that

- most major currencies belong to an identifiable group or bloc of currencies, and
- exchange rates between currencies in the same bloc are much more stable than exchange rates between currencies in different blocs.

Many currencies are closely tied in value to the dollar, and some are fairly closely linked to the euro.

The exchange rates of currencies within each bloc have greater stability than exchange rates between currencies in different blocs. Relative stability is achieved largely by central bank policy in each country, e.g. on interest rates, and intervention in the markets to support weaker currencies. Governments link their currency to another currency (the host currency) for one of two main reasons

- to defend the competitive position of the country's products either in export markets denominated in the host currency, or in markets where they face competition from host country manufacturers
- to stimulate international trade within a trading bloc comprising several countries.

The Hong Kong dollar, for example, has been held at a rate of around $1 = HK$7.80 for several years to protect the competitive position of Hong Kong manufacturers in the US market, and to compete with US manufacturers in markets outside the US.

If the assumption about exchange rate stability is valid, companies can utilize currency blocs for transaction-based structural hedging between two or more currencies in the same bloc. This strategy is sometimes referred to as cross matching of currencies.

Income in one currency can be matched against expenditures in a different currency in the same bloc. Currency risk should be low because there should be little variation in the exchange rate between the two currencies.

*Example*

A company that sells into the UK market in dollars and sources its goods in Hong Kong can offset the two currency flows (dollar income and Hong Kong dollar payments) against each other as a structural hedge because both currencies are in the dollar bloc. This avoids the cost of hedging the economic exposure in the foreign exchange markets. It would be necessary, however, to exchange the currency of the receivables (in this case dollars) into the currency of the payables (Hong Kong dollars) by means of a spot or forward sale in the foreign exchange markets, in order to pay Hong Kong suppliers out of the dollar income stream.

# Summary

Transaction-based structural hedging can be an effective and cheap hedge against currency exposures. However, matching of income and payments in the same currency is often difficult to achieve. Companies might earn income in a currency but make no payments, or might have payments in a currency but no income. Matching normally will be partial because incomes and expenditures in any currency will not be exactly the same.

Cross matching income and expenditure in different currencies within the same currency bloc is effective as a hedging technique only for as long as there is a reasonable degree of exchange rate stability between currencies in the bloc.

# 4

# Strategic Structural Hedging

Strategic structural hedging is a method of hedging economic exposures. There is no complete hedge against economic exposures for an international company, but it is possible to create structural hedges, and to some degree

- create a long-term match between currencies of revenue and of cost, and
- match the company's cost structure (in currencies) with those of its major competitors.

# Strategic Issues

A company's treasury department can advise its board of directors about strategic hedges but cannot take much direct action because structural remedies are not its responsibility. They involve issues such as

- In which countries should operations be based?
- Should production be moved from one country, where costs are high, labor is inefficient and prospects for the economy and the domestic currency are poor, to another country where the outlook is more favorable?

One reason a Japanese manufacturer might transfer production facilities to the US or the UK would be to reduce its exposure to adverse changes in the dollar/yen rate and the sterling/yen rate and of course the euro/yen rate too.

An international company might have manufacturing facilities in several countries, and depending on exchange rate movements, it would be able to switch production from one country to another, as a hedge or as a means of benefiting from the rate changes. Such an approach normally can be adopted for long-term changes only in relative currency levels because there is a cost in rescheduling production between existing plants unless of course spare capacity exists in all the company's plants. Transferring production to a new plant also would result in high costs, both in equipping the plant and training the workforce.

# Purchasing Power Parity (PPP) Theory

The purchasing power parity (PPP) theory is that in the longer term the exchange rate between the currencies of two countries will alter in relation to their respective rates of inflation. The PPP rate is the exchange rate between two currencies at which there is competitive parity in costs of production in each of the two economies. For example, if a basket of goods representing a typical spread of manufactured products costs \$1,500,000 in the US and an identical basket of goods costs £1,000,000 in the UK, the sterling/dollar PPP rate is £1 = \$1.50. At that exchange rate UK manufacturers would be broadly competitive with their US counterparts.

Now suppose that the sterling/dollar PPP rate is originally £1 = \$1.50 and is identical to the market exchange rate, at a time when the retail price index in both countries is 100. In the following two years, however, the price index has risen to 110 in the US and to 120 in the UK. The higher rate of inflation in the UK should, according to PPP theory, cause sterling to weaken against the dollar, and the exchange rate will fall to \$1.50 x 110/120 = £1 = \$1.375.

Exchange rates don't follow PPP predictions in the short term, as is evident from their large short-term fluctuations, but over time, PPP theory could be a fairly reliable indicator of changes in exchange rates. The PPP rate is significant in that it represents competitive parity between two currencies towards which the market exchange rate should ultimately gravitate, in a free currency market.

If a currency is valued significantly above or below its PPP rate against other currencies, for a substantial period of time, the economic implications could be far-reaching. During the late 1990s, sterling's value against the dollar was significantly above its PPP rate against other leading currencies. As a consequence, UK manufacturers had much greater difficulty in exporting domestically produced goods at a reasonable profit level. Doubts have been expressed about the appropriate level at which sterling might eventually enter the single currency system of EMU: if the value of sterling were to be fixed at a high level relative to the euro, UK producers might struggle to compete against other European producers.

For a UK firm incurring production costs in sterling, but exporting its products and pricing them in dollars, the implications of a strong pound in relation to the dollar have been as follows:

- non-UK competitors, especially US producers, would gain a long-term cost competitive advantage from an appreciation in the value of sterling against the dollar, and so
- a strategic response would be to close down production facilities in the UK and open them in the US or in a country in the dollar bloc.

This response might seem an extreme solution to the problem. However, a strategy of shifting production facilities has two main advantages.

- It puts the UK producer in the same economic terrain with existing competitors from dollar bloc countries, thus removing the advantages that those competitors would otherwise enjoy because of an undervalued dollar and overvalued sterling.
- It is an effective hedge against economic exposures. If the currency exposures are large, this action can safeguard the survival of the company.

Some UK-based multinationals have made such strategic decisions to hedge their economic exposures. At worst, such a strategy could cost the closure and re-siting of production facilities, and loss of profits if the sterling/dollar exchange rate moved in favor of UK-based producers, with sterling weakening and the dollar strengthening. At best, however, the company should survive in its markets and retain its competitive edge.

*Example*

Developments in the early 1990s at UK-based Rolls-Royce illustrate the vulnerability of a company with a single-country manufacturing base competing in a price-sensitive multinational market. General Electric and Pratt & Whitney, both of the US, are its main rivals in the market for jet engines and jet-engine spare parts. By early 1991, the combination of intense competition, successful cost-cutting by its rivals, the worldwide economic recession and a weak dollar meant that Rolls-Royce found its profit margins under pressure.

The head of the supply group at Rolls-Royce at the time indicated that part of the answer was to source more work overseas: "Our competitors do, and if we don't, we'll lose out."

An advantage of sourcing any product in the dollar-based Asian countries is the dramatically lower labor costs compared with the US. This would enable companies such as Rolls-Royce to create a structural currency hedge as well as its competitive advantage against its rivals.

# Summary

Strategic structural hedging is a longer-term option for the multinationals operating in global markets. Unlike transactions-based structural hedging, it is not a solution to short-term currency exposures.

# 5

# Hedging with Forward Contracts

A forward exchange contract is an agreement between a customer and a bank for the purchase or sale of a specified quantity of one currency in exchange for another, at a fixed rate of exchange and for settlement at a future date. The future settlement date, specified in the contract, is either a specific date (for an outright forward contract) or any time between two specified dates (for a value-date option contract). This chapter looks at forward contracts as a hedging instrument for currency exposures.

# Locking in an Exchange Rate

Forward exchange contracts are the most commonly used instrument for currency risk hedging by non-bank corporates. They are used to lock in an exchange rate for a future purchase or sale of currency. If there is an underlying business transaction, a forward contract will eliminate the currency exposure because the rate of exchange for the future transaction is fixed, regardless of changes in the spot rate between the contract date and settlement date.

*Example 1*
A US company knows that in three months' time, it must pay a German supplier €100,000 for goods. The current spot rate of exchange is €1 = $0.65 and because the company will have to buy euros with dollars to make the payment, it expects its cost to be £65,000 (100.000 ÷ 0.65). The company has already sold the goods to a US customer for $70,000 and expects to make a $5,000 profit.

*Analysis*

If the company is concerned about its exposure to the payment of €100,000 in three months' time, it is because the euro might strengthen against the dollar and erode the profit margin. For example, if the spot rate after three months were €1 = $0.67, it would cost $67,000 (100,000 ÷ 0.67) to buy the euros and the profit on the transaction would be just $3,000.

A forward contract would eliminate this risk. If the three-month forward rate were €1 = $0.66, purchasing €100,000 would cost $66,000 (€100,000 ÷ 0.66) and the company would secure a profit of $4000. (There are no additional transaction costs associated with arranging a forward contract.)

*Example 2*

A US company sells goods to an Italian customer who insists on paying in euros and in three months' time. The company expects its costs of sale to be $100,000, and it wants to be sure of a profit of at least 25% on the transaction. The current euro/dollar spot rate is €1 = $0.65 and the three-month forward rate is €1 = $0.64.

*Analysis*

If the company bases its selling price on the spot rate, it will charge its customer €192,307 ($125,000/0.65). However, the eventual dollar income from the €192,307 will depend on what the spot rate is in three months' time, and the company is at risk from a decline in the value of the euro against the dollar during the three-month exposure period.

By setting a price of €195,312 ($125,000 x 0.64) and arranging a forward contract to sell this currency at €1 = $0.64 in three months, the company would lock in revenue of $125,000 and a profit of $25,000, having eliminated its currency exposure.

A forward contract is a binding contract that commits the counterparties to buy and sell the agreed amounts of currency. Exchange rates can move either way, adversely or favorably. Locking in an exchange rate for a future cash flow therefore avoids the downside effects of an adverse movement in the spot rate but also removes the possibility of profiting from a favorable movement.

*Settlement Date*

Settlement date (value date) for a forward contract can be arranged for any bank working day to suit the customer's requirements. However, for forward contracts with a maturity of a given number of months (one month, two months, six months, etc.) settlement date is determined from the spot value date.

Spot value date is two working days from the transaction date. A two-months forward contract would be settled two calendar months after spot value date (or on the last working day of the month).

If today's date were Monday April 3, settlement of a two-month forward contract would be on Monday June 5.

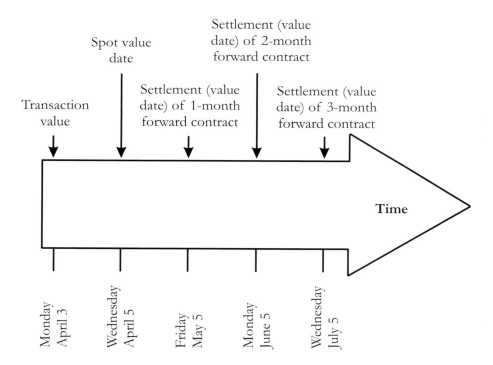

# The Forward Rate

The forward rate differs from the current spot rate by an amount reflecting interest rate differentials between the two currencies.

For example, if the current dollar/New Zealand dollar spot rate is $1 = NZ$1.72, and the one-year interest rate is 5% for the dollar and 6% for the New Zealand dollar, the one-year forward rate would be obtained as follows

|  | Variable (quoted) currency | | Base currency |
|---|---|---|---|
|  | NZ$ |  | $ |
|  | 1.7200 | = | 1.0000 |
| Interest for one year (6%) | 0.1032 | (5%) | 0.0500 |
| After one year | 1.8232 | = | 1.0500 |
| One-year forward rate |  | = | 1.8232/1.05 |
|  |  | = | $1 = NZ$1.7364 |

The difference between the spot rate and the forward rate is known as the forward adjustment or forward points. In the example above, the variable currency (the New Zealand dollar) is quoted forward against the dollar at a value below its spot price, and the forward adjustment is NZ$0.0164 (164 points).

A formula for calculating the forward adjustment is

$$\text{Forward points} = \frac{S \times \dfrac{I_V - I_B}{100} \times \dfrac{D}{360^*}}{1 + \left[\dfrac{I_B}{100} \times \dfrac{D}{360^*}\right]}$$

(* 365 when the base currency is sterling, the Australian dollar or the Irish punt.)

where

$S$ = the spot rate

$I_V$ = the interest rate on the quoted (variable) currency

$I_B$ = the interest rate on the base currency

$D$ = the number of days to the forward contract's maturity.

In the previous example, the forward points for a one-year forward contract could be calculated as follows

$$\frac{1.7200 \times \dfrac{6-5}{100} \times \dfrac{360}{360}}{1 + \left[ \dfrac{5}{100} \times \dfrac{360}{360} \right]} = \frac{0.0172}{1.05} = 0.0164$$

The value is positive; therefore the forward points should be added to the spot rate to obtain the forward rate of 1.7364 (1.7200 + 0.0164).

Because the forward points reflect the interest rate differential between the two currencies, the forward adjustment normally is larger for longer-dated forward contracts than for shorter-dated contracts, to reflect the increase in rolled-up interest differentials over time.

Although the forward rate can be either more or less favorable than the spot rate, comparing the current spot rate with a forward rate to see which is more favorable has little practical meaning. A company does not choose between buying or selling at today's spot rate and arranging to buy or sell at a forward rate at some time in the future. The choice is really between

- doing nothing yet, waiting until the time of the currency receipt or payment, and then buying or selling at whatever the spot rate happens to be, or
- eliminating the currency exposure by arranging a forward contract for the time of the expected receipt or payment.

A forward rate is not a prediction of what the future spot rate will be. For example, if the sterling/dollar spot rate is £1 = $1.50, and the one-month forward rate is $1.495, it would be wrong to assume that the foreign exchange markets expect the dollar spot rate to strengthen to

$1.495 over the month. Rather, $0.005 would reflect the value of the difference between dollar and sterling interest rates over a one-month period. However, if a currency is quoted forward against the base currency at a higher value, its spot rate is more likely to strengthen in value over the forward period. Similarly, if a currency is quoted forward against the base currency at a lower value, its spot rate is more likely to weaken in value over the forward period.

When forward points are quoted for the bid and offer rates, if the forward points for the bid rate are higher than for the offer rate, the quoted (variable) currency has a higher value forward than spot. Deduct the forward points from the spot rate to obtain the forward rate. If the forward points for the bid rate are lower than for the offer rate, the quoted (variable) currency has a lower value forward than spot. Add the forward points to the spot rate to obtain the forward rate.

| | | |
|---|---|---|
| Bid rate – forward points | | Offer rate – forward points |
| If bid rate forward points offer rate forward points, | > | deduct the forward points |
| If bid rate forward points offer rate forward points, | < | add the forward points |

*Exercises*

To check your understanding of forward contracts as a hedging instrument, try to complete the following exercises. The appropriate forward rates should be taken from the table below and the solutions follow each exercise.

*Pound Spot - Forward Against the Pound*

| | Spot | Three-month forward adjustment | Six-month forward adjustment |
|---|---|---|---|
| US | 1.5010-1.5016 | 1.77-1.75 | 3.28-3.24 |
| Sweden | 12.2645-12.2845 | 5¼ -6 | 8-9 |

*Exercise 1*

A company has a fixed price contract to supply goods and services to a customer for £1.25 million. Its costs are expected to be £600,000 in sterling plus $700,000 for work sub-contracted to an overseas supplier. The payment to the supplier will be made in six months' time. The company would like to ensure a profit of at least £180,000 and is worried about the volatility of the sterling/dollar rate.

What profit can the company lock in by arranging a forward contract now, on the assumption that its sterling costs are £600,000?

*Solution*

The company must pay $700,000 in six months and so will buy dollars to make the payment. The six month forward rate is

| | |
|---|---|
| Spot rate (bid rate) | 1.5010 |
| Forward adjustment (six months) | -0.0328 |
| Forward rate | 1.4682 |

The bank will quote the rate more favorable to itself, which is the lower of the bid and offer rates for selling the quoted currency. The forward points should be subtracted because the adjustment is higher for the bid rate (3.28) than for the offer rate (3.24).

| | £ |
|---|---|
| Sterling costs of the business contract | 600,000 |
| Cost of buying $700,000 at forward rate (÷ 1.4682) | 476,774 |
| Total costs | 1,076,774 |
| Sales value of contract | 1,250,000 |
| Profit | 173,226 |

The company can achieve a profit of about £173,000, not as much as it had hoped. If it decides not to arrange a forward contract, however, it will have a $700,000 dollar exposure for six months, and the actual profit on the contract will depend on the spot rate on payment date.

*Exercise 2*

A company is arranging a contract to sell equipment to a customer in Sweden. The customer wants to pay in three months from the date of the contract, and insists on paying in krona. The company expects its costs to be $500,000.

By arranging a forward contract for the krona income, what would the company's profit be if it agreed a sales price of SKr7.5 million?

*Solution*

In three months' time the company will receive SKr7.5 million that it will sell for dollars. The bank will offer a forward rate of

| | |
|---|---|
| Spot (offer rate) | 12.2845 |
| Forward adjustment (three months) | +0.0600 |
| Forward rate | 12.3445 |

The bank will quote the rate more favorable to itself, which is the higher of the bid and offer rates for buying the quoted currency. The forward points are added to the spot rate because the forward adjustment is lower for the bid rate ($5^1/_4$) than the offer rate (6).

| | $ |
|---|---|
| Income (SKr7.5 million ÷ 12.3445) | 607,558 |
| Costs | 500,000 |
| Profit | 107,558 |

The company can lock in a profit of $107,558 by arranging a forward contract. If it does not hedge its exposure to the krona income, it will be at risk from a fall in the value of the krona over the next three months, and its actual profit could be lower.

# Value Date Option Contracts

If a company is uncertain about deciding the value date for settlement of a forward contract, it can arrange a contract that gives it the option to settle at any time between two specified dates.

*Example*

A UK company expects to receive $500,000 at some time during May, but is not sure when. It is now late February. The company's finance director is concerned about the risk of a depreciation in the value of the dollar, and would like to lock in an exchange rate for converting the dollar income into sterling.

Spot and forward rates available for February 27 are as follows

| | |
|---|---|
| Spot (£/$) | 1.5025-1.5035 |
| Two months forward | 2.24-2.27c |
| Three months forward | 3.15-3.18c |

Spot value date is Wednesday March 1.

*Analysis*

The company can lock in a forward rate by arranging a forward contract to sell $500,000, for value at any time between Monday May 1 and Thursday June 1.

The bank will quote either the two-month forward rate or the three-month forward rate, whichever is the more favorable to itself.

| | Two month forward rate | Three month forward rate |
|---|---|---|
| Spot rate (offer rate) | 1.5035 | 1.5035 |
| Forward adjustment (add) | 0.0227 | 0.0318 |
| Forward rate | 1.5262 | 1.5353 |

The bank will be buying the quoted currency (dollars) and the higher offer rate of 1.5353 is the more favorable. The forward rate for a contract for value at any time between May 1 and June 1 therefore will be $1.5353, and the company can guarantee itself sterling income of £325,669 from the $500,000.

# Closing Out a Forward Contract

A forward contract hedges a currency risk when there is an underlying transaction creating the exposure. A company also could arrange a forward contract to hedge a transaction that either does not happen or happens earlier or later than expected. In such situations, the forward contract becomes a currency exposure instead of a hedge, and the company will make a profit or loss on currency trading, depending on the exchange rate during the exposure period. When a forward contract is arranged as a hedge for a transaction that does not materialize, the bank will close out the forward contract by making a reverse sale or purchase of currency at the spot rate.

*Example*
A German company expects to receive $204,000 on April 7. On January 5 it arranges a three-month forward contract for the sale of these dollars into euros (for a value date of April 7). The forward rate obtained is €1 = $1.02. In April, the US customer fails to pay the amount due.

*Analysis*
The company must honor its contract to sell $204,000 to the bank at $1.02, but has no dollars to sell. The bank therefore will close out the forward contract.

A close-out can be arranged by means of a spot transaction on April 5 (spot value date April 7). The bank will close out the forward contract by

- selling dollars spot to the company, and
- buying them back at the forward rate of $1.02.

In other words, the company must fulfil its forward contract obligations, and the bank provides the currency in a new FX transaction to enable the forward contract to be honored.

Because the same amount of dollars is being sold and purchased for settlement on April 7, no actual exchange of dollars is necessary, the sale and purchase cancel each other out. There will be a settlement in euros for the difference in the rate at which the two transactions are made.

If the spot rate for the new transaction is less than $1.02, the company will make a loss on the close-out. For example, if the spot rate is $1.005, the loss will be

| | € |
|---|---|
| Sale of $204,000 at forward rate (÷ 1.02) | 200,000.00 |
| Purchase of $204,000 spot (÷ 1.005) | -202,985.07 |
| Loss on close-out | -2,985.07 |

If the spot rate for the purchase is above $1.02, the company will make a profit on the close-out. For example, if the spot rate is $1.03 the profit will be

| | € |
|---|---|
| Sale of $204,000 at forward rate (÷ 1.02) | 200,000.00 |
| Purchase of $204,000 spot (÷ 1.03) | -198,058.25 |
| Profit on close-out | +1,941.75 |

Although close-out could result in a profit, it could also result in a loss. This is because currency risk is two way, with the profit or loss depending on which way the exchange rate moves. Because the forward contract is closed out, and because there is no underlying transaction, the company has had an exposure for the purchase of $204,000 over the forward contract period. Instead of being a hedge, the forward contract has caused the exposure.

The close-out of a contract need not happen on the settlement date. In this example, if the company knows before April 5 that the US customer will refuse to pay, it could ask its bank to close out the contract immediately. This would be done by arranging for the company to purchase $204,000 at a forward rate for settlement on April 7. The basic analysis, however, remains the same in that between the time of the original forward contract and its close-out, the company has had a currency exposure for a dollar purchase, created by the forward contract and the absence of an underlying transaction.

# Extending a Forward Contract

A forward contract can be extended or rolled forward when the underlying transaction is delayed beyond the settlement date for the forward contract. For example, a Spanish company might arrange a two-month forward contract to sell $1 million as a hedge against an anticipated receipt of that amount. Subsequently, if the dollar income is not received for a further six weeks, the company could extend the forward contract for the new date.

When a bank agrees to extend a forward contract, however, it is actually arranging a forward swap by which it

- closes out the old contract, and
- arranges a new contract, with the rate adjusted to reflect the interest rate differential between the two currencies for the additional period of time.

# Uncertain Amounts of Currency

When a forward contract is arranged to cover a specific future receipt or payment of a known quantity of currency, the currency exposure will be hedged completely. In some instances, however, the amount of a receipt or payment might be uncertain, although its timing is known or predictable. For example, a company might have regular receipts or payments in a currency as part of its normal trading operations. It knows that it will receive or pay some currency every week or every month, but doesn't know exactly how much each time. In these circumstances management could decide to arrange a partial hedge through forward contracts.

*Example*
A company sells goods abroad regularly, receiving income in sterling, dollars and euros. Its cash budget for the next three months anticipates the following receipts

|           | January      | February     | March         |
|-----------|--------------|--------------|---------------|
| Sterling  | £600,000     | £400,000     | £900,000      |
| Dollars   | $1 million   | $500,000     | $1.5 million  |
| Euros     | €900,000     | €300,000     | €2 million    |

These are estimates, but the company believes that January receipts in each currency will be at least 90% of the budget, and February and March receipts will be at least 80% and 60% of budget respectively. The company would like to use forward contracts to hedge its currency income exposures during this period.

*Analysis*

If the company arranges forward cover for more than its eventual income, it will create a currency exposure for itself. For example, suppose it arranged a forward contract to sell $1 million in January, perhaps by means of a value-date option contract, giving the company the option to sell dollars at the same fixed rate at any time during the period covered. If actual income in dollars is only $900,000, the company will have an exposure to a dollar payment of $100,000 because eventually it will have to buy this amount (at spot rate) to close out the contract.

Management could choose a partial hedge, with forward cover for either the minimum expected currency income, or for an amount between the minimum and the budget figure. Therefore forward contracts could be arranged for

- $900,000 and €810,000, to cover 90% of budgeted currency receipts in January
- $400,000 and €240,000, to cover 80% of budgeted receipts in February
- €900,000 and €1.2 million, to cover 60% of expected receipts in March.

Any surplus income could be sold at the spot rate towards the end of each month.

# Period of Forward Cover

How far in the future a forward contract can be arranged depends on the willingness of banks to agree to a contract lasting beyond a certain time for a given currency. The forward market is less liquid in some currencies than in others, and is less liquid for longer time periods ahead. For example, large companies and banks are able to arrange forward cover for dollars against sterling or euros, in New York or London, for settlement dates up to five or more years ahead. Banks would not agree to such long-dated contracts for smaller companies that they would regard as a greater credit risk. In many currencies, forward cover will be difficult to arrange for a settlement date more than two years, or perhaps even one year ahead. Most forward contracts are for dates up to six months ahead, and so are predominantly used to hedge short-term currency exposures.

*Choosing the Period of Forward Cover*

To fully hedge an exposure, the forward contract should be timed to coincide with the underlying transaction cash flow. For example, if a company expects to pay SFr100,000 on May 5, the forward contract to buy Swiss francs should be arranged for delivery on May 5.

However, the treasury department of a large company might not always seek full hedging. Instead, it might take a speculative view on future short-term interest rates in two currencies, and the time period for a forward rate contract is then based on this view. The purpose is to try to secure a more favorable exchange rate while taking a fairly low risk.

*Example*

The sterling/dollar spot rate is 1.4975. The forward adjustments for forward contracts are

| | |
|---|---|
| 6 months | 2.70c |
| 1 year | 4.90c |

The interest rate on the dollar is lower than the interest rate on sterling and so the dollar is quoted forward at a higher value than its spot rate.

A large company is expecting to receive $10 million in one year's time, and its treasury department believes that interest rate differentials between sterling and the dollar will be as wide, or wider, in six months as they are now, so that the forward premiums on the dollar will remain as large or perhaps become larger.

*Analysis*

Instead of arranging to sell $10 million one year forward, the company might decide to sell the $10 million just six months' forward, and after six months ask the bank to extend the forward contract by a further six months, to the end of the one-year period. Suppose that after six months, the spot rate is unchanged, but the forward adjustment is larger, as follows

| | |
|---|---|
| Spot | $1.4965-1.4975 |
| Six month forward | 2.80c-2.70c |

If the company had arranged a one year forward contract, the income from selling $10 million at $1.4485 (1.4975 - 0.0490) would have been £6,903,693.

By arranging to sell $10 million just six months' forward, at an exchange rate of 1.4705 (1.4975 - 0.0270), the company contracted to receive £6,800,408 after six months, but would then ask the bank to extend the contract by a further six months.

In the extension of the contract, the bank would sell $10 million spot at perhaps $1.4970 (the mid price of the bid and offer rates), for £6,680,027 and extend the forward contract six months to buy $10 million at 1.4700 (1.4970-0.0270) for £6,802,721.

*Summary of Example*

| After six months | £ |
|---|---|
| Company sells $10 million at 1.4705 | + 6,800,408 |
| Extension: company buys $10 million at 1.4970 | - 6,680,027 |
| After 12 months, company buys $10 million at 1.4700 | + 6,802,721 |
| Overall net income | +6,923,102 |

By successfully speculating on the interest rate differential between the dollar and the sterling, the company has earned about £19,000 more for the $10 million than it would have done if it had arranged a one year forward contract.

# 6

# Currency Options

A currency option is an arrangement between an option holder (the buyer) and an option writer (the seller). It gives the holder the right, but not the obligation, either to buy or sell a quantity of one currency in exchange for another at a specified rate of exchange, known as the strike price or strike rate or exercise price. The option to buy or sell must be exercised on or before a specified expiry date, typically several months from the date the option is written. When a holder exercises the option, the option writer must comply with its terms, and buy or sell the currency at the specified strike price. Options lapse if they are not exercised by their expiry date.

## Features of Currency Options

Options are available from two sources. Over-the-counter (OTC) options are arranged individually with a bank. Traded options are purchased through a broker on an options exchange, such as the Philadelphia Stock Exchange (PHLX). There are also options on currency futures: using currency futures for hedging is described in a later chapter.

*Calls and Puts*
A call option gives its holder the right to buy the specified quantity of currency at the strike price. A put option gives its holder the right to sell the currency.

*Quantity of Currency*

The quantity of currency that the option holder can buy or sell is specified in the option agreement and is for an amount specified by the option buyer. OTC options usually are for fairly large amounts, typically from $2 million to $20 million. Therefore they are unsuitable for small companies wishing to hedge fairly small transaction exposures.

For exchange-traded options, the quantity is a standard amount. On the Philadelphia Stock Exchange, for example, sterling options (against the dollar) are for £31,250 each. If a company wishes to obtain an option to sell £125,000, it would have to buy four sterling puts (4 x £31,250 = £125,000). Currency options traded on the PHLX are

| Against the dollar | Quantity per option |
|---|---|
| Sterling | £31,250 |
| Australian dollar | A$50,000 |
| Canadian dollar | C$50,000 |
| Swiss franc | SFr62,500 |
| Yen | ¥6,250,000 |
| Euro | €62,500 |
| *Cross-rate options* | |
| Deutschemark/yen | DM62,500 |
| Sterling/deutschemark | £31,250 |

*American and European Options*

With a European option, the holder can exercise the option on its expiry date but not before. With an American option, the option can be exercised at any time up to and including its expiry date. Both styles of option are available over-the-counter and exchange traded.

American options would be preferred when the holder is uncertain about the exact date of an underlying transaction for which the option is being used as a hedge. For example, if a UK company expects to receive $5 million between the end of April and the end of May, that it will sell for sterling, it could arrange an American OTC put option with a bank to sell the dollars at any time up to May 31 so that the option can be exercised, if required, as soon as the dollars are received. With a European option, the company would have to wait until May 31, regardless of when the dollars are received, if it wished to exercise the option.

American options cost more to purchase than similar European options.

*Strike Price*

The strike price is the rate of exchange at which the currency will be bought (call option) or sold (put option) if the option is exercised. When the option is written, the strike price might be higher, lower or exactly the same as the rate currently available in the FX markets.

Options are said to be at-the-money when their strike price is the same as the exchange rate that could be obtained for an FX transaction in the cash market.

- An American style option, that can be exercised at any time up to expiry, is at-the-money if its strike price is the same as the current spot rate of exchange. (The option is at-the-money-spot or ATMS.)
- A European-style option, that can be exercised on its expiry date only, is at-the-money if its strike price is the same as the rate for a forward exchange contract maturing on the option's expiry date. (The option is at-the-money-forward or ATMF.) When a European option reaches expiry it is at-the-money if the strike price equals the current spot rate on the expiry date.

An option is in-the-money when its strike price is more favorable to the option holder than an at-the-money strike price. An option will be exercised only when it is in-the-money.

An option is out-of-the-money when its strike price is less favorable to the option holder than an at-the-money strike price. An out-of-the-money option will not be exercised, because the option holder would do better to arrange the currency purchase or sale by means of a spot FX transaction.

The amount by which an option is in-the-money or out-of-the-money will vary over time with changes in the exchange rate. An option that is out-of-the-money or at-the-money when written could become in-the-money on or before expiry.

The option buyer can decide what strike price he wants. For an OTC option, an exact strike price can be specified. Exchange-traded options are available at any of several strike prices (some in-the-money and some out-of-the-money) that are set by the options exchange. Out-of-the-money options are cheaper than in-the-money options.

*Examples*

An American call option to buy Swiss francs (SFr) for euros is in-the-money by SFr0.03 per €1 when the strike price is €1 = SFr1.63 and the spot rate is €1 = SFr1.60, because it would be cheaper to buy Swiss francs at the option strike price.

An American put option to sell yen for sterling is out-of-the-money by ¥2.00 per £1 when the strike price is £1 = ¥158.00 and the spot rate is £1 = ¥160.00, because selling yen at the option strike price would earn less than selling them at the current spot rate.

*Premiums*

The buyer of an option must pay a premium to the seller (the option writer). The premium is the price the seller wants to receive in exchange for taking on the currency risk. The risk is that the option holder will exercise the option, and that the option writer will make a loss on the difference between the strike price and the spot rate of exchange on the exercise date.

The amount of the premium for an option therefore will depend on the option writer's perception of the risk of making a loss, and a higher premium will be charged when the risk seems greater that the option will be exercised.

OTC options are slightly more expensive than similar exchange-traded options, because of the bank's administrative costs in negotiating terms that are tailor-made to the customer's requirements. OTC option premiums are not publicized, but typically are 1%-5% of the amount of currency involved, for ATMF options in major currencies with a maturity of up to one year.

# Hedging with Options

Currency options might be a suitable method of hedging a currency exposure for the *option buyer*, who can

- lock in a worst possible exchange rate to avoid the risk of an adverse rate movement, and at the same time
- benefit from any favorable rate movement by choosing not to exercise the option, and instead buying or selling the currency at the spot rate on expiry.

If currency options are bought to hedge a currency exposure, the buyer must feel

- the risk reduction justifies the premium cost
- an option is preferable despite its cost compared to other alternatives, such as the (zero-cost) forward exchange contract.

*OTC Options*
OTC options are often a more convenient method of hedging for companies than traded options because an option can be negotiated to match exactly the exposure, for the amount of currency and the expiry date. (However, the Philadelphia Stock Exchange also trades customized options as well as standard options. Customized options give their buyers greater flexibility than standard traded options.)

*Example 1*
A French company expects to make a payment of $3 million in one

month's time, on September 8. The current forward rate for value September 8 is €1 = $1.02, and the cost of the dollars at this rate would be €2,941,176. The company suspects that the dollar will weaken against the euro and wants to benefit from this; therefore it does not want to arrange a forward exchange contract. On the other hand, it would like to ensure that the maximum cost of the dollar payment is around €3 million (an effective exchange rate of €1 = $1).

*Analysis*

The company might consider a call option on $3 million (to buy dollars in exchange for euros). The worst possible exchange rate that the company is trying to secure is parity (€1 = $1) for buying the dollars, but the cost of the option premium should be taken into account. The bank might offer to write a European call option on $3 million with a strike price of perhaps $1.015, for expiry on September 6 and settlement on September 8. The premium might be €40,000. This option would be out-of-the-money by one cent (1.02-1.01).

If the company agrees to buy an option on these terms, it would lock in a worst possible exchange rate of $1.015 for its purchase of the dollars. The cost of the premium should be added, however, to calculate the effective worst case exchange rate.

|  | € |
|---|---|
| Purchase of $3 million at 1.01 (option exercised) | 2,955,665 |
| Premium | 40,000 |
| Maximum cost | 2,995,665 |

The effective exchange rate is €1 = $1.0014 ($3 million ÷ €2,995,665)

The company's objective of an exchange rate no lower than $1.00 has been achieved.

The call option gives the company the chance to benefit from favorable movements in the euro/dollar rate. For example, if the spot rate on September 6 is €1 = $1.03, the company would let the option lapse and buy the $3 million it needs for €2,912,621. Adding the premium for the option, the company's all-in cost would be just €2,952,621.

When an OTC option is arranged between a bank and a non-bank customer, it is usual to provide for cash settlement rather than physical exchange of currencies, in the event that the option is exercised. In this example, if the option is exercised on September 6, the bank will pay the company for the difference in the value of $3 million at the strike price of $1.015 and its value at the current spot rate. The company would then arrange a spot transaction to buy the dollars for delivery on September 8 (spot value date).

*Example 2*
A UK company expects to receive ¥200 million in six months' time (by the end of October). The current spot rate is £1 = ¥160. The company thinks the yen is likely to strengthen in value during the next few weeks, but also it would like to hedge against a drop in the yen. It therefore considers an American put option on ¥200 million, with an expiry date of October 29 and settlement two days after exercise of the option. The company suggests a strike price of £1 = ¥165 (that is out-of-the-money by five yen) for which the bank quotes a premium of £20,000. The company accepts and buys the option.

*Analysis*
The company has locked in a worst-possible exchange rate of £1 = ¥165. Allowing for the cost of the premium, the worst possible outcome will be

|  | £ |
|---|---|
| Put option exercised, sale value of ¥200 million at £1 = ¥165 | 1,212,121 |
| Premium cost | -20,000 |
| Net proceeds | 1,192,121 |

This gives an effective worst-possible exchange rate for the yen income of £1 = ¥167.77 (¥200 million ÷ £1,192,121).

The put option will be exercised if the spot rate is above 165. If the spot rate is below 165, perhaps at 156 when the yen income is received, the company would let the option lapse and sell the yen at the spot rate to earn £1,282,051 (200 million ÷ 156). After deducting the premium cost of £20,000, this would give net revenue of £1,262,051, representing an effective exchange rate for the transaction of 158.47.

*Exchange-Traded Options*
Exchange-traded options might be more suitable for hedging than OTC options when a company or bank has large, regular but uncertain cash flows, and is therefore less concerned with the exact quantity of the currency of exposure. Traded options are convenient and flexible because they are easily bought and sold.

*Example 1*
A German company expects to receive $4 million in December and wishes to hedge the currency exposure with traded options from the Philadelphia Stock Exchange. It wishes to sell dollars and buy euros, consequently it will have to purchase call options on euros. The current euro/$ spot rate is €1 = $1.05, and the company opts for a strike price of $1.04 that is in-the-money. At this strike price, the cost of European-style December € call options is 2.24 cents per euro.

*Analysis*
The company wishes to sell $4 million for euros. At a strike price of 1.04, this has a euro value of €3,846,154 ($4 million ÷ 1.04). The call options are on euros and are for €62,500 each, so that the company will have to buy 62 euro FX options contracts to obtain full cover for its currency exposure (€3,846,154 ÷ €62,500 per option contract = 61.5 contracts).

The cost per option is $1,400 (€62,500 x 2.24 cents per euro), thus the cost of 62 options will be $86,800.

The option strike price is $1.04. If the spot rate on the exercise date in

December is higher than 1.04, the company will exercise its options and buy euros (sell dollars) at this strike rate, receiving €3,846,154 in exchange for $4 million.

If the spot rate is below 1.04 on the exercise date, the company will let the options lapse and sell the dollars (buy euros) at the spot rate. Income from the $4 million will exceed €3,846,154. (For example, if the spot rate is 1.01, the $4 million could be sold for €3,960,396.)

The cost of ensuring a rate not worse than €1 = $1.04, by purchasing the options, is the $86,800 needed to buy them.

*Example 2*
A UK company has to pay $14.9 million in March. It wishes to ensure that the maximum total sterling cost will be £10 million (a cost of £1 = $1.49) in order to guarantee a minimum profit on a trade contract. It wants to use exchange-traded options to limit its exposure. The spot £/$ rate on January 23 is 1.5655-1.5665.

Because the company wishes to buy dollars and sell sterling, it can purchase sterling put options on the Philadelphia Stock Exchange for expiry in March. The strike rate should be one that will secure a worst-possible rate of 1.49, net of premium, to keep costs at no more than £10 million. For a strike price of 1.5250, the premium is 3.36 cents per £1, giving a net rate of £1 = $1.4914.

*Analysis*
At a strike price of 1.5250, the $14.9 million has a sterling equivalent value of £9.77 million. Each sterling-traded option is for £31,250, and so the company would have to buy 312.66 put options (£9.77 million ÷ £31,250 per contract) to cover the exposure exactly. But because fractions of options cannot be purchased, the company might decide on 312 options. This would give it the right to sell £9.75 million at 1.525 for $14,868,750, and so there is a remaining exposure from the original $14.9 million of $31,250. The company might decide to leave this exposure unhedged and buy these dollars at the spot rate in March.

The premium for 312 contracts would cost $327,600 (312 contracts x 3.36 cents x £31,250). The company could pay this premium by purchasing he dollars spot (at 1.5655) for £209,262.

*Outcome 1*
If the spot rate is above the strike rate, at 1.55 for example, when the option expires in March, the company will buy the $14.9 million spot.

| | £ |
|---|---|
| Cost of spot purchase (at 1.55) | 9,612,903 |
| Cost of premiums for options | 209,262 |
| Total cost | 9,822,165 |

This is within the maximum cost limit of £10 million. The effective rate obtained is £1 = $1.5170 ($14.9m ÷ £9,822,165).

*Outcome 2*
If the spot rate is below the strike rate, at 1.50 for example, when the option expires in March, the company will exercise its options.

| | £ |
|---|---|
| Exercise options at 1.525 (strike rate) | 9,750,000 |
| Purchase $31,250 (in sterling, unhedged) at spot rate of 1.50 | 20,833 |
| Cost of premiums | 209,262 |
| Total cost | 9,980,095 |

This is within the maximum target cost limit of £10 million. The effective rate obtained is £1 = $1.4930 ($14.9m ÷ £9,980,095).

Whatever the dollar spot rate is on expiry date, the company's cost should be within its maximum limit of £10 million.

# An Alternative to Forward Contracts

As we have seen, forward exchange contracts are widely used for hedging a currency exposure because they lock in a fixed exchange rate for a future foreign currency transaction. Currency options provide an alternative method of hedging. It would be possible, for example, to buy a currency option with a strike price equal to the currently available rate for a forward contract, so that the option holder would secure an exchange rate that is at worst the same as the forward rate. The advantage of an option over a forward contract lies in the choice of *not* exercising the option if the spot exchange rate moves in the holder's favor before the exercise date. The option holder could then buy or sell the required currency in the spot market at this better rate, allowing the option to lapse.

A European-style option with an at-the-money-forward (ATMF) strike price will work out cheaper than a forward exchange contract for a specific transaction if

- the spot price at maturity is more favorable than the strike price, so that the option is not exercised
- the amount by which the option holder benefits from buying or selling currency at this spot rate exceeds the premium paid for the option.

*Example*
A company has to pay a German supplier €3 million in six months' time. The company wishes to hedge the euros exposure with either a forward contract or a European-style euro call option at a strike price of €1 = £0.65. The rate for a six month forward contract also would be €1 = £0.65. The cost of the option premium would be £70,000.

*Analysis*
The cost of buying the euros with a forward contract would be £1,950,000 (3,000,000 x 0.65). Using a currency option could cost more or less, depending on whether the option is exercised. The benefit of an option would come from not having to exercise it if the spot rate falls below 0.65.

| Spot rate at expiry date | | Call option | Forward contract |
|---|---|---|---|
| | Premium | 70,000 | |
| €1 = £0.70 | Cost of euros (option exercised) | 1,950,000 | |
| | Total cost | 2,020,000 | 1,950,000 |
| | Premium | 70,000 | |
| €1 = £0.65 | Cost of euros (spot) | 1,950,000 | |
| | Total cost | 2,020,000 | 1,950,000 |
| | Premium | 70,000 | |
| €1 = £0.60 | Cost of euros (spot) | 1,800,000 | |
| | Total cost | 1,870,000 | 1,950,000 |

The breakeven spot rate, at which the call option would be less expensive than a forward contract, would occur when the cost of buying the €3 million equals the cost at the strike price/forward rate, minus the cost of the option premium.

This breakeven spot price is

$$\frac{£1,950,000 - 70,000}{€3,000,000} \quad = \quad 0.6267$$

At any spot rate below 0.6267, on the exercise date, the option would be cheaper than the forward contract.

The diagram on page 68 illustrates the comparative costs of a forward contract and a call option for the same expiry date, as well as the same strike price for the option and the forward rate.

A company purchasing an option instead of arranging a forward contract would be assuming that exchange rate movements could be large, and that the eventual spot rate is likely to be more favorable than the current forward rate. Unless the exchange rate is volatile, the cost of an option premium usually will make at-the-money forward options more expensive than forward contracts.

Volatility in exchange rate movements can add to the hedging appeal of currency options. Greater volatility, though, is likely to mean higher premiums for the purchase of options, reflecting the higher risks to which a writer of options is exposed.

**Costs: Buying call options vs forward contract**
**where strike price = forward rate**

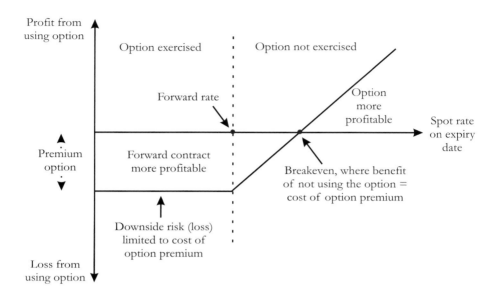

*Exercise*

A company expects to receive $6 million in six months' time that it will want to convert into sterling. It arranges a six month dollar put option at a strike price of £1 = $1.50, that is the six month forward rate for dollars. The option premium is 1.5 pence per dollar.

What would the spot sterling/dollar rate need to be in six months for the overall cost of hedging with an option to be the same as hedging with a forward exchange contract?

*Solution*

*Forward contract.* The company would commit itself to selling the $6 million (at 1.50) for £4 million.

*Option.* The cost of the premium would be £90,000 ($6 million x £0.015 per $1). The put option gives the company the right to sell $6 million at 1.50 to earn £4 million.

The benefit of an option over a forward contract is the holder's ability to let it lapse and use the spot market if the exchange rate moves favorably. In this case, breakeven will occur if the option holder lets the option lapse and sells the $6 million at the spot rate to earn £4,090,000 (4 million + 90,000). The breakeven spot rate is therefore 1.4670 (6 million ÷ 4,090,000).

If the spot rate falls below this level, a currency option will be more profitable than a forward contract because income from selling the $6 million spot (and letting the option lapse) will exceed £4,090,000.

# Potential Currency Exposures

Currency options can be much more attractive than forward contracts when there is uncertainty about whether a future currency receipt or payment will actually occur.

If a company thinks that it will have to pay $5 million in three months' time, it can arrange a forward contract to buy $5 million. But if the payment isn't actually needed, the company is still obliged to buy the $5 million. Instead of hedging a currency exposure for a dollar payment, it has taken on an exposure for a $5 million purchase. Forward contracts create such exposures, in situations where future currency receipts or payments might not occur. Currency options get round this problem. For the cost of the premium, a company can

- let the option lapse if the receipt or payment doesn't occur
- let the option lapse if the receipt or payment does occur, but the spot rate is more favorable
- exercise the option if the receipt or payment does occur, and the strike price is more favorable than the spot rate
- exercise the option if the receipt or payment does not occur and the strike price is more favorable than the spot rate that would give the company a profit.

Even if the receipt or payment does not occur, but the strike price is more favorable than the spot rate, the company could make an immediate profit by exercising the option and arranging a reverse transaction at the spot FX market rate.

- For a call option, the option holder could exercise the right to purchase the currency at the strike price and sell it immediately at the higher spot rate.
- For a put option, the option holder could buy currency at the spot rate to coincide with exercising the right to sell it at a higher strike price.

(In practice, if the holder of an OTC option is not a bank, the bank writing the option usually will settle its obligations when the option is exercised by means of a cash settlement for the difference between the strike price and the current spot rate. Consequently there is no need for the option holder to arrange a spot FX transaction because the profit comes from the cash settlement.)

Currency options might be used by a company that has tendered a price for a contract in foreign currency. A put option to sell the currency could be exercised in the event that it wins the contract and earns the currency, but allowed to lapse otherwise. However, covering tender-to-contract risk with currency options would make sense only if the chances of winning look good. Too many unsuccessful tenders, all covered by currency options, would result in high – and wasted – premium costs.

# Uncertain Amounts of Currency

Options also can be more attractive when the future amount of foreign currency income or expenditure is uncertain. Arranging forward contracts could in these circumstances create currency exposures rather than hedge them, in much the same way as if the foreign currency receipt or payment didn't happen at all. For example, if a company expects to receive about $3 million in six months, but is not certain of the exact amount, it might arrange a forward contract to sell $3 million.

However, there will be a currency exposure for the amount by which actual receipts exceed or fall short of the $3 million. Currency options could be used to hedge the exposure for the uncertain amount of currency income or spending.

*Example*
A company with dollar exports estimates that its income in three months' time will be at least $5 million and possibly as much as $7 million or more. It could

- arrange three-month forward cover to sell $5 million
- purchase a three-month dollar put option for $2 million
- deal with any other surplus (or deficit) in dollar income through spot transactions.

This use of currency options can be valuable for hedging uncertain currency exposures where companies issue overseas price lists in foreign currency.

# Limitations of Options

Options have some drawbacks as a hedging instrument.

- *Cost.* Regular use of options will involve high premium costs. The holder must be satisfied that these costs justify the risk being hedged. A user of exchange-traded options also must pay brokers' commission.
- *Period of cover.* Options are mainly for short-term exposures. Traded options are available with expiry dates up to 12 months ahead. A bank might agree to a longer-dated OTC option, up to two years (possibly longer in some cases) for very good customers.
- *Currencies.* Only a limited number of currencies are available in traded options. OTC options can be arranged for any convertible currencies, provided a bank is willing to write such an option.

# Summary

Both OTC and traded currency options can be used to hedge currency exposures or to speculate on future changes in spot prices. They can be more attractive than forward contracts

- where exchange rates are volatile
- for potential currency exposures
- for currency exposures of an uncertain amount.

# Tender-to-contract Cover

When a company tenders for an overseas contract, it often has to quote a price in a foreign currency. In doing so, it creates a potential exposure to foreign currency income. Whether or not the currency exposure will actually happen depends on whether or not the company wins the contract. If it wins, the potential exposures become actual exposures, and appropriate methods can be used to hedge them.

A potentially serious risk will exist, however, during the period between tendering and winning or losing the contract. This risk is that the currency in which the bid has been made will weaken during the tender-to-contract (TTC) period. For example, if a UK company bids for an overseas contract in dollars and estimates that its costs will be £12 million, it might quote a price of $20.40 million on the assumption that the exchange rate will be £1 = $1.50, a rate at which it could arrange forward contracts for the contract period. The contract therefore would be expected to earn £13.6 million in income and a profit of £1.6 million. However, because the exchange rate is likely to change during the tender-to-contract period that could be several months, the planned profit is at risk. If the dollar were to weaken to $1.70 for example, during this period, the contract would earn only £12 million at the tendered price, and the expected profit would be eliminated by the exchange rate movement.

The tender price could be increased to allow for a possible fall in the value of the foreign currency in the tender-to-contract period, but raising the price could mean losing out to a rival bidder.

A company should limit its potential currency exposures for large contracts because an adverse exchange rate movement could damage profits. Hedging either with forward contracts or currency options is often not suitable.

- Forward exchange contracts would create a currency exposure if the tender were unsuccessful.
- Premium costs for options will be high if the company tenders frequently and fails to win the contracts.

A hedging instrument for companies tendering for major contracts abroad is called tender-to-contract cover (TTC). In the US this is provided by banks and OPIC.

There are similar agencies in other countries offering similar services. In the UK it is the Export Credits Guarantee Department (ECGD), in France it is COFACE, in Holland it is NCM, and in Germany it is HERMES.

# Bank Tender-to-contract Cover

A company about to bid in a foreign currency for an overseas contract could arrange TTC cover from its bank for a specific amount of currency and a specific period of time. The agreement fixes a rate of exchange.

- The company must accept this exchange rate if the contract is won. Even if the spot exchange rate has moved in the company's favor by this time, it must accept the rate fixed in the cover agreement.
- If the contract isn't won, the cover agreement lapses.

The company must pay a premium for the cover, but this is not as high as for currency options.

*Example*
A company is about to bid $8 million for an overseas contract and asks its bank for TTC cover for up to three months, the time needed for a

decision. For a premium, the bank agrees to give TTC cover at an exchange rate of £1 = $1.50 (that might be the three month forward rate for dollars). The bank is providing a guaranteed fixed rate of exchange for the contract income, in the event that the contract is won, regardless of future movements in the spot rate during the tender-to-contract period.

If the company doesn't win the contract, its total hedging cost is the cost of the premium. If it does win, it must sell its $8 million income to the bank at £1 = $1.50, regardless of the forward rate when the contract is awarded or the spot rate when the contract revenue of $8 million is eventually received that might be months or even several years later.

# Credit Insurance Agency
# Tender-to-contract Cover

Tender-to-contract cover also is available from credit insurance agencies. It is similar to bank coverage, but has existed longer.

Credit insurance agency cover is intended to help exporters in their home country bidding for capital goods contracts or construction projects with a high domestic cost element, i.e. over $15 million, where the contract price is in a foreign currency and the company submitting the tender is obliged to quote a firm price. Only the domestic content of a contract can be covered, and it is available only for contracts priced in certain currencies (currencies with well-developed forward exchange markets): dollars, yen, Swiss francs, Canadian dollars, Danish kroner, Norwegian krone, Swedish krona and the euro.

Under credit insurance agency cover, an exporter is guaranteed an exchange rate for up to nine months. For longer TTC periods, guaranteed rates are reset every nine months. A company wishing to obtain TTC cover should ask the credit agency for a schedule of guaranteed forward rates for the currency in which the tender will be submitted.

If the contract is won, the exporter arranges to sell its currency income forward to a bank and informs the credit agency of the forward rate obtained.

- If the forward rate is less favorable than the guaranteed rate, ECGD will pay the difference, provided it exceeds 1% of the guaranteed income, and up to a maximum 24% of the guaranteed income. The exporter carries the first 1% loss (= 1% of the domestic content of the contract price) and the credit agency's maximum liability is 24%.
- If the forward rate is more favorable than the guaranteed rate, the company's surplus income must be paid over to the export credit agency.

Credit insurance agency tender-to-contract cover, unlike that offered by banks, also requires the company to seek basic credit insurance cover (against default risk for up to 90% of the contract amount).

The premiums payable for TTC cover from these agencies are designed to make the bulk of the risk premium payable only if the tender is successful.

- There is an initial premium, non-refundable, equal to 0.01% of the amount of cover (subject to a minimum premium). This is payable when the schedule of guaranteed forward rates is issued.
- If the tender is accepted and a contract is signed, there is a further non-refundable premium payable of 0.4% of the amount guaranteed. This *unwinding* premium covers the risk that, for whatever reason, the supply contract will not become effective and so the forward exchange contracts now entered into by the company will need to be unwound.
- The main premium becomes payable only when the company receives the first payment from the customer under the export contract. The amount of premium varies between 2.5% and 4.1%, depending on the length of the TTC period. The initial premium is set off against the main premium.

*Example*

A company that tenders for a contract at a price of $30 million seeks ECGD tender-to-contract cover. The guaranteed forward rate offered is £1 = $1.50, and so the sterling value of the tender is £20 million. The initial premium is £5,000 (minimum charge).

*Analysis*

*Outcome 1*

If the tender is unsuccessful, no further premium is payable.

*Outcome 2*

If the tender is successful and the contract is signed, the company will enter into suitable forward exchange contracts with its bank. A non-returnable premium of £80,000 (0.4% of £20 million) is then payable.

When the customer makes the first down-payment under the contract, the main premium becomes payable. If the TTC period were, for instance, just over four months, the premium would be 3.3%.

|  | £ |
|---|---|
| Main premium payable (3.3% of £20 million) | 660,000 |
| Less initial premium already paid | 5,000 |
| Payment | 655,000 |

Let's suppose for simplicity that the forward exchange contracts entered into by the company were all at £1 = $1.60. The sterling value of the contract income will be £18.75 million ($30 million ÷ 1.60). ECGD has guaranteed a rate of £20,000,000.

|  | £ |
|---|---|
| Total loss (20 million - 18.75 million) | 1,250,000 |
| First 1% loss borne by company (1% of £20m) | 200,000 |
| ECGD liability | 1,050,000 |

In this example, the company will have benefited by a net £310,000 (£1,050,000 - £80,000 - £660,000) by taking out TTC cover.

# TTC Cover via Currency Options

As explained in the previous chapter, a company can arrange its own cover for the tender-to-contract period via currency options. While the front-end premium normally will be higher than for branded TTC cover, self-arranged cover does have the following advantages

- Greater liquidity. It is difficult to arrange coverage in excess of about $35 million of a major currency with a bank or credit insurance agancy. If the currency is considered exotic, i.e. a non-major currency, there is little chance of finding a provider of TTC cover.

- Scope for profit if the tender fails. Option cover can be terminated at a profit if the tender is rejected, depending on the movement in the underlying currencies during the tender period. Such profit could partially or wholly offset the cost of the abortive tender or even represent a windfall profit if the tender costs are modest. In contrast, dedicated TTC cover lapses if the tender is unsuccessful and provides no potential for profiting from a beneficial exchange rate move during the tender period.

# Currency Loans and Deposits

In some situations, borrowing or investing currency on deposit can be useful methods of hedging currency *transaction* exposures.

# Hedging Transaction Exposures

A company could have difficulty arranging a forward exchange contract to hedge a transaction occurring in the long term. Banks are often reluctant to arrange forward contracts with a maturity date a year or more ahead, except in heavily traded currencies such as the dollar, the euro, the yen and sterling, but a company could either borrow or deposit the specified currency to create the hedge.

- For a future payment, a hedge can be created by purchasing the currency now at the spot rate and depositing the money until the due payment date.
- For a future receipt, the company could obtain a loan in the particular currency and convert it into the company's domestic currency at the spot rate. The eventual currency receipt would be used to repay the loan.

*Example*
A company will be required to make a payment of 26.25 million Swedish kronas (SKr) in one year, and would like to hedge this exposure. It is unable to arrange a one-year forward contract in kronas. The interest rate on 12-month krona deposits is 5%, and the $/SKr spot rate is $1 = SKr8.5.

*Analysis*

A hedge against the exposure can be created by purchasing kronas now and depositing them for one year at 5%. To have SKr26.25 million on deposit after one year, including accumulated interest, the company would need to deposit SKr25 million now (SKr26.25 million ÷ 1.05). The purchase of SKr25 million would cost $2.941 million.

A hedge against the exposure to the future payment of SKr26.25 million has been created because the SKr purchased now and placed on deposit will be sufficient to make the scheduled payment in one year.

The spot purchase of the kronas fixes the rate at which the payment will be made. However, if the company has to borrow dollars to buy the kronas spot, there will be the additional interest cost of servicing the dollar loan. The interest rate differential between the kronas deposit receipts and the dollar loan should equate with the premium or discount to the spot rate (the forward points) for a forward contract, had such a contract been obtainable.

Similar hedging arrangements can be made as an alternative to forward contracts for transactions in the near future and in currencies in which a forward exchange contract would be available if preferred.

*Example*

A UK company will receive $60,900 in three months' time and wants to hedge this exposure. The spot exchange rate is £1 = $1.60 and the interest on a three-month dollar loan would be 6% per annum.

*Analysis*

The company can create a hedge by borrowing dollars now for three months and converting them into sterling. The loan plus interest will be repaid out of the dollar income after three months, and the loan therefore has provided an exact hedge for the exposure to dollar receivables.

Interest for three months would be $1^1/2$% (6% x $^3/_{12}$) and to create a hedge for the $60,900 receivables the dollar loan will have to be $60,000 ($60,900 ÷ 1.015).

The company therefore should borrow $60,000 and convert this into sterling to obtain £37,500 at the spot rate of 1.60. The currency exposure has been fully hedged because after three months, the loan plus interest, totalling $60,900, will be paid out of the dollar income, and £37,500 has been obtained for the dollars three months in advance.

*Summary*

|  | $ | £ |
|---|---|---|
| *Now* | | |
| Borrow $60,000 | +60,000 | |
| Sell for sterling | -60,000 | +37,500 |
| *In three months' time* | | |
| Dollar income | + 60,900 | |
| Repay loan with interest | - 60,900 | |

# Factored Foreign Debts

An exporting company might use a factor (factoring company) to collect its overseas debts. The factor will collect the money due from the exporter's customers, and pass on receipts (less fees and commissions) to the exporter. A factor will also lend against the security of invoiced and unpaid export debts.

A company with overseas debts in foreign currencies that uses the services of a factor could partially hedge its exposures to its currency receivables by

- borrowing in currency from the factor, and
- repaying the loan out of eventual receipts from the overseas customers.

*Example*
A company might sell goods regularly to Singapore priced in Singaporean dollars (S$) and use a factor to collect the debts. Sales are

S$300,000 each month, and customers have one month's credit. The factor agrees to lend the company 70% of outstanding unpaid debts.

*Analysis*
There would be a series of one month loans of S$210,000 (70% of S$300,000) and the dollars would be converted into sterling. The loan would be repaid out of the eventual dollar income and therefore would provide a 70% hedge for the company's exposure to Singapore dollar receivables.

# Comparison with Forward Contracts

Loans and deposits are more flexible than forward contracts because amounts borrowed or deposited and repayment periods can be changed. Forward contracts, in contrast, are binding agreements. On the other hand, interest costs are uncertain for variable rate borrowing. For currency loans and deposits to provide an exact hedge for a currency transaction exposure, the interest rate should be fixed for the period of the exposure.

Both borrowing and forward contracts will use up a company's credit lines. Borrowing, however, has 100% weighting in the bank's calculation of credit lines utilisation, whereas exchange contracts have a lesser weighting by banks because the default risk is considered lower.

If a company has currency borrowings or deposits at the end of its financial year, it will have a translation exposure. Forward contracts, in contrast, are off-balance-sheet items and do not create such an exposure.

In summary, currency loans represent a flexible means of hedging foreign currency exposures and also a method of meeting funding requirements. The flexibility and cost of currency borrowing can be compared with alternative hedging options, such as forward contracts, and then used as appropriate.

# Currency Futures

A currency future is a contract for the sale or purchase of a standard quantity of one currency in exchange for another currency at a specified rate of exchange, and for delivery at a specified future time, normally in March, June, September or December. They are bought and sold on a futures exchange, the largest being the International Monetary Market division (IMM) of the Chicago Mercantile Exchange (CME). They allow financial institutions, investors and companies to trade in exchange rate risk, and can be used to hedge currency exposures.

# Buying and Selling Futures

Most currency futures are for a major currency against the dollar. On the CME, there are futures contracts for a number of currencies against the dollar including contracts in sterling, Australian dollars, Canadian dollars, yen, Swiss francs and euros.

A buyer of a sterling future is contracting to buy sterling in exchange for dollars. The seller of a sterling future is contracting to sell sterling in exchange for dollars. When a futures contract is bought and sold, the price is the agreed exchange rate. For example, when an investor buys a March sterling future at 1.4500, this (£/$) rate is both the agreed rate for the exchange of sterling into dollars in March and also an expression of the current market price of the futures contract.

- If the market price subsequently goes up before the March delivery date, the buyer of the future will benefit and the seller will suffer a loss.

## TRADING IN EXCHANGE RATE RISK

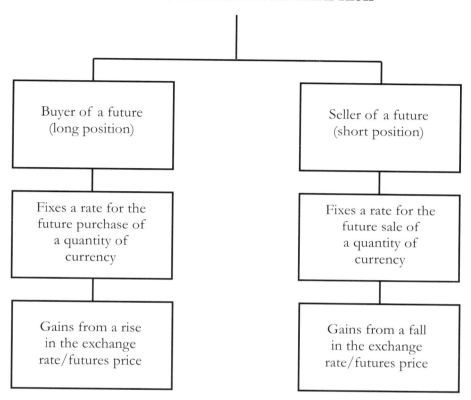

- If the market price falls, the seller of the future will gain and the buyer will suffer a loss.

*Example*
A sterling December future is bought by an investor on the CME at 1.5500. The futures price subsequently goes up to 1.5600.

*Analysis*
A sterling future is for £62,500 against the dollar. A contract was purchased by the investor at 1.5500. The current market price is established by the exchange authorities at the end of each day, i.e. the contract is marked-to-market, so that all gains or losses on futures

positions can be monitored. The investor, having bought a future, is long in sterling and will gain from any rise in the value of sterling against the dollar.

The change in price is 100 points and the gain to the buyer (and loss to the seller) can be measured as follows

CME sterling future: standard quantity £62,500

|  | $ |
|---|---|
| Cost of buying £62,500 at contracted rate of 1.5500 | 96,875 |
| Current value of £62,500 at current rate of 1.5600 | 97,500 |
| *Gain to buyer* from price change of 100 points | 625 |

The gain to the buyer is $6.25 for each one point increase in the market price. This is also the loss incurred by the seller of the future.

The gain or loss from a movement in a futures price is a standard amount for each point or tick of movement. On the Chicago Mercantile Exchange, the value per point is as follows for some of the currency futures traded. Amounts and values are in dollars.

| Future | Quantity of currency | Price quotation | Amount of one point in price | Value of each one point change in price |
|---|---|---|---|---|
| British pound | £62,500 | $ per £1 | $0.0001 | $6.25 |
| Australian dollar | A$100,000 | $ per A$1 | $0.0001 | $10 |
| Canadian dollar | C$100,000 | $ per C$1 | $0.0001 | $10 |
| Yen | ¥12,500,000 | $ per ¥1 | $0.000001 | $12.50 |
| Swiss franc | SFr125,000 | $ per SFr1 | $0.0001 | $12.50 |
| Euro | €125,000 | $ per €1 | $0.0001 | $12.50 |

Although currency futures can be held until maturity (delivery date), when the currencies are exchanged, futures positions normally are unwound before delivery.

- A buyer of a future can unwind his position by selling a future for the same delivery date, taking a cash gain or loss on the difference between the buying and selling price.

● Similarly, a seller of a future can unwind the position by purchasing a future for the same delivery date, taking a cash gain or loss on the difference between the selling and buying price.

*Example*
A company buys six December euro FX futures on the CME at a price of 1.04 (€1 = $1.04). Subsequently it unwinds its position by selling six December euro FX contracts when the price has risen to 1.05.

*Analysis*
The company has realized a cash profit of 100 points per contract (1.05 - 1.04) and its total profit is

| | |
|---|---|
| Value per point | $12.50 |
| Number of points profit per contract | 100 |
| Number of contracts | 6 |
| Total profit ($12.5 x 100 x 6) | $7,500 |

# Hedging with Futures

Futures can be used for hedging currency exposures, particularly for large amounts of currency, as an alternative to a forward contract. Such hedging usually would involve

● the purchase or sale of futures to cover a future currency transaction
● unwinding the futures position when the transaction occurs
● buying or selling the physical currency in the spot FX markets.

Hedging with futures is easier for US companies because the dollar is their domestic currency and futures are available for all major currencies against the dollar.

- If a US company expects to make a foreign currency payment at a future date, it could arrange a forward contract to buy the currency; alternatively it could buy futures.
- If a US company expects to receive currency income at a future date, it could arrange a forward contract to sell the currency; alternatively it could sell futures.

For non-US companies, opportunities to use futures might be more restricted, except for transactions involving the dollar. A UK company, for example, that is expecting to make a payment in dollars could use a forward contract to buy the required dollars; alternatively it could use CME futures by *selling* sterling futures because selling sterling also would mean buying dollars. The UK company would have more difficulty using futures to hedge its exposures in Swiss francs for example, because of the limited number of futures contracts for cross-rate currencies, i.e. exchange rates not involving the dollar, such as sterling/Swiss francs.

*Example 1*
A UK company wants to hedge a dollar exposure. It expects to receive $2 million in late May from a customer and wants to fix a rate for selling the dollars for sterling. It could arrange a forward contract at a £/$ rate of around 1.50, but prefers to use CME futures. The price of June sterling futures is 1.50.

*Analysis*
To hedge its $2 million exposure, the company will want to sell dollar receipts (and buy sterling) and so should buy sterling futures. The transaction will occur in late May, and the appropriate futures contract normally will be for the next delivery date which in this example is June.

Each sterling future on the CME is for £62,500 and at a price of 1.50, the dollar equivalent is $93,750. The company could buy 22 June sterling futures at 1.50 (purchasing £1,375,000 in exchange for $2,062,500). The hedge is not for the exact amount of the exposure of $2 million.

When the company receives its dollar income of $2 million in May, it could keep the dollars until the June settlement date for the futures contract.

However the company is more likely to unwind its position when it receives the dollar income in May, and sell 22 June sterling futures.

*Outcome 1*

Suppose that the market price for the futures at this time is 1.4825 and that the spot sterling/dollar exchange rate is 1.4850. In this situation there will be a loss on the futures trading.

|  | $ |
|---|---|
| Purchase price of futures | 1.5000 |
| Sale price of futures | 1.4825 |
| Loss per future | 0.0175 |

The total loss for 22 contracts at $6.25 per point is $24,062.5 (22 x 175 x $6.25).

The company's position is as follows

|  | $ |
|---|---|
| Receive dollars (cash transaction) | 2,000,000.0 |
| Loss on futures trading | 24,062.5 |
| Net dollars received | 1,975,937.5 |

These can be sold at the current spot rate (1.4850) to earn £1,330,598. The effective exchange rate for the $2 million receivable is therefore 1.5031 ($2 million ÷ £1,330,598), which is close to the rate of 1.50 that the company was seeking as a hedge when it bought the futures.

*Outcome 2*

Suppose the futures price had been above 1.50 in May at 1.53 and the spot rate had been 1.5250. There would have been a gain of 300 points per futures contract or $41,250 for the 22 contracts.

The company's position would be as follows

|                                      | $         |
|--------------------------------------|-----------|
| Receive dollars (cash transaction)   | 2,000,000 |
| Profit on futures trading            | 41,250    |
| Total dollar receipts                | 2,041,250 |

These can be sold at the spot rate (1.5250) to earn £1,338,525. The effective exchange rate for the $2 million receivable is therefore 1.4942 ($2 million ÷ £1,338,525). This is close to the rate of 1.50 that the company was seeking as a hedge for its dollar exposure.

Unwinding a position in a liquid futures market gives the user total flexibility on timing.

*Example 2*
A UK company expects to make a payment of $1.45 million to a supplier in August. The company wishes to use CME sterling futures to hedge its exposure, and the current price for September sterling futures is 1.4500.

*Analysis*
The company will want to buy dollars (sell sterling) in August to make the payment, and so it should sell sterling futures. At a rate of £1 = $1.45, the sterling equivalent of $1.45 million is £1 million. 16 futures would represent £1 million exactly, so the company should sell 16 September sterling futures at 1.4500.

Suppose that when the dollar payment is due in August, the spot rate of exchange is 1.4150 and the September futures price is 1.4100. The company would unwind its position by purchasing 16 September futures.

It will have made a profit from the fall in the exchange rate because it held a short position, i.e. as a seller in sterling futures.

$

| Original selling price for futures | 1.4500 |
|---|---|
| Purchase price for 16 September futures to unwind position | 1.4150 |
| Profit per contract on unwinding position | 0.0350 |

The profit of 350 points per contract at $6.25 per point, and for 16 futures contracts, gives a total cash profit of $35,000.

| | $ |
|---|---|
| Dollar payment due to supplier | 1,450,000 |
| Profit from futures trading | -35,000 |
| Dollars to be purchased (balance) | 1,415,000 |
| Spot rate of exchange | 1.4150 |
| Sterling cost of dollar purchase | £1,000,000 |

Ignoring commission charges to the futures broker, the effective exchange rate for the payment of $1,415,000 is exactly 1.45 ($1.45 million ÷ £1 million). This is the exchange rate that the hedging arrangement with futures was intended to secure.

*Exercise*

Check your understanding of futures as a hedging instrument by attempting the following exercise.

A company expects to pay €7.5 million to a supplier in February and wishes to use CME futures to hedge this exposure. It is concerned that the euro could strengthen against the dollar in the period between now and February.

- The current price of March euro FX futures is 1.0350. Each futures contract is for €125,000. How should the company use futures as a hedge for its currency exposure?
- When the payment is due in February, the price of March euro FX futures is 1.0450. The current spot rate of exchange is €1 = $1.0425. How should the company unwind its position and what would be the effective exchange rate for the euro

HEDGING CURRENCY EXPOSURES

payment? (Each point or tick for a euro FX futures contract is worth $12.50.)

*Solution*

- The company wishes to buy euros to hedge its exposure, and so should buy euro FX futures. Sixty futures contracts would represent €7.5 million, therefore the company should buy 60 euro FX contracts for delivery in March at a price of 1.0350.
- The futures position would be unwound in February by selling 60 March contracts at 1.0450.

| | |
|---|---:|
| Purchase price of contracts | 1.0350 |
| Sale price of contracts, to unwind position | <u>1.0450</u> |
| Profit per contract | 100 |

A profit of 100 points per contract, for 60 contracts and at $12.50 per point, gives a total profit of $75,000.

The €7.5 million must be purchased at the spot rate of €1 = $1.0425, giving a purchase cost of $7,818,750. The net cost to the company, allowing for the profit of $75,000 on futures trading, is $7,743,750. The effective exchange rate for the purchase of the €7.5 million is therefore €1 = $1.0320. This is close to the rate of 1.0350 that the company was trying to fix by using futures to hedge.

# Hedging with Futures: Advantages and Disadvantages

The following table summarizes the main advantages and disadvantages of using futures as a hedging instrument. It should be noted that smaller companies do not normally use futures to hedge their currency exposures, in particular because they don't properly understand what they are or how they work.

## Hedging with Futures

| Advantages | Disadvantages |
|---|---|
| The purchase of futures does not affect a company's credit lines with its bank | Commission payable to a futures exchange broker |
| Opportunity to profit from favorable exchange rate movements | A cash deposit (a margin or performance bond) must be paid to the broker by both buyers and sellers of futures, and no interest is receivable on this. Margin positions are monitored and top ups might be necessary. A company purchasing futures contracts could be asked to pay such variation margins several times in the same week if market prices are moving unfavorably |
| Positions can be unwound at any time because of the large and liquid market, thus giving timing flexibility for hedging | Available for standard contract sizes and for standard delivery dates only; creating an exact hedge therefore is very difficult and some basis risk is unavoidable |
| | Administration and monitoring can be burdensome |
| | Exposures normally can be hedged for short periods only (up to 12 months) |

# Currency Swaps

A swap is an agreement between two parties for the exchange of a stream of cash flows over a specified term. One of the parties to the contract is normally a specialist bank. Currency swaps involve the exchange of a stream of cash flows in one currency for a stream of cash flows in a different currency.

# Elements in a Swap

A currency swap consists of three or sometimes just two main elements.

- There is an exchange of principal at the beginning of the swap. One party gives the other a quantity of one currency in exchange for a second currency at an agreed rate of exchange, normally at or close to the current spot rate. One of the two currencies involved is commonly the dollar.

- At regular intervals, normally six monthly or annually, there is an exchange of payments. It is convenient to think of these as interest payments on the swapped amounts of principal, although swaps are not loans. The amount to be exchanged by each party is calculated at a swap rate (interest swap) on the amount of principal exchanged. This might be a fixed rate or a floating rate.

- At the end of the term of the swap, there is a re-exchange of the principal amounts, with each party repaying the currency that was received at the start of the swap period. The rate of exchange is therefore exactly the same as for the initial exchange of principal.

Many currency swap agreements do not involve a physical initial exchange of principal at the start of the swap, just a notional exchange on nominal amounts of each currency.

Start of swap (near-value date):

Initial exchange of principal at £1 = $1.60

Many swaps do not involve an exchange of principal at the start of the swap term. If the parties wish to obtain the currency they can buy it in the spot FX market.

Interest exchange (six-monthly):

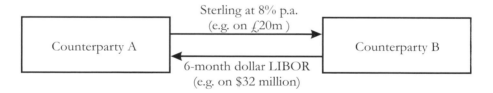

End of swap (fair-value date):

Re-exchange of principal

# Hedging with Swaps

Currency swaps are long-term instruments, typically with a term of between two and 10 years. Therefore as a hedging instrument, they are appropriate only for longer-term exposures. These can arise in a number of ways

- with foreign currency loans
- with foreign currency investments
- when an organization expects a large currency payment or receipt in two years' time or longer.

*Foreign Currency Loans*

A company might have a foreign currency loan that is creating a currency exposure. The exposure would arise from the interest payable on the loan and the eventual requirement to repay the loan principal at maturity. A swap would provide a hedge by means of an exchange of cash payments from the currency of the exposure into a second currency, perhaps the company's domestic currency.

**Without a swap**                **With a swap**

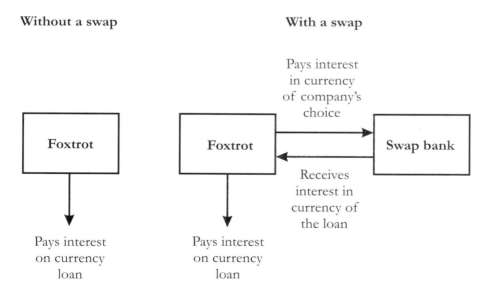

*Example*

Two years ago, a UK company, Foxtrot, incurred a five-year debt in dollars. The debt was for $100 million, repayable at par at the end of the loan term, with interest payable annually at 8%. The dollar debt was incurred to finance an investment in New York that has been sold. Foxtrot therefore has a currency exposure to its dollar loan repayment and its dollar interest payments, and would like to create a hedge.

| Year | Hedge required Debt payments | = income |
|------|:---:|:---:|
| | $ | $ |
| 1 | -8 million | +8 million |
| 2 | -8 million | +8 million |
| 3 | -8 million | +8 million |
| 3 | -100 million | +100 million |

The current spot rate of exchange is £1 = $2.

*Analysis*

The company might be able to arrange three forward exchange contracts, to buy $8 million, $8 million and $108 million at the end of Years 1, 2 and 3 respectively.

Alternatively, it could arrange a currency swap, with a notional, not an actual, exchange of principal at the near-value date. Let's presume that a bank's swap rate for paying fixed dollars is 5% per annum and for receiving fixed sterling is 10% per annum.

The bank would calculate the cost to itself, in present value terms applying the swap rate of 5% per annum, of paying the required dollar cash flows in each of the three years. The calculation is

| Year | Swap payment (bank to Foxtrot) | Discount at 5% | Present value |
|------|-------------------------------|----------------|---------------|
|      | $ |  | $ |
| 1 | 8 million | ÷ 1.05 | 7,619,048 |
| 2 | 8 million | ÷ $(1.05)^2$ | 7,256,236 |
| 3 | 8 million | ÷ $(1.05)^3$ | 6,910,701 |
| 3 | 100 million | ÷ $(1.05)^3$ | 86,383,760 |
|   |  |  | 108,169,745 |

At an exchange rate of £1 = $2, the present value of the bank's dollar payments under the swap would have an equivalent sterling value of £54,084,873. The bank would stipulate that under the terms of the swap there would be a notional exchange of $108,169,745 for £54,084,873 at the start of the period.

- The bank would pay dollars at 5% per annum, and be willing to provide this money as $8 million after the first year, $8 million after the second year and $108 million after the third year.
- In return, Foxtrot must make payments to the bank based on a notional principal of £54,084,873 and a swap rate of 10%, possibly as follows

| Year | Swap payment (Foxtrot to bank) | |
|------|-------------------------------|--|
|      | £ | |
| 1 | 5,408,487 | (interest) |
| 2 | 5,408,487 | (interest) |
| 3 | 5,408,487 | (interest) |
| 3 | 54,084,873 | (principal) |

The swap exchange can be summarized as follows, showing that Foxtrot, by using swap receipts to service its dollar loan, has exchanged a dollar liability for a sterling liability, and so hedged its dollar exposures. Its dollar receipts from the swap will be used to meet its payment obligations under the dollar loan agreement.

| Year | Swap cash flows Foxtrot receives | Foxtrot pays |
|---|---|---|
| | $ | £ |
| 1 | 8 million | 5,408,487 |
| 2 | 8 million | 5,408,487 |
| 3 | 108 million | 59,493,360 |

*Foreign Currency Investments*

In a similar way, an asset swap could be used in a situation where a company has a currency exposure arising from the future income stream from a foreign investment. The company could arrange a swap in which it makes payments in the currency of exposure to match the receipts, and in exchange receives a stream of income in the currency of its choice.

*Long-dated Currency Transactions*

Occasionally, a company might expect a large receipt or payment in a foreign currency in several years' time. It could try to hedge the exposure with a forward contract, but a long-dated contract might be unobtainable. A currency swap can be a surrogate long-dated forward contract.

*Example*

Echo, a UK company, expects to receive $30 million from a foreign government in two years' time. It wishes to hedge the exposure, but is unable to arrange a forward contract. A bank is willing to make a swap agreement on the following terms

● a notional exchange of $30 million for sterling at £1 = $1.50
● annual exchanges of interest at fixed rates of 10% on sterling and 5% on the dollar
● an exchange of principal after two years at the end of the swap.

This example has been simplified, to make the analysis more clear.

*Analysis*

The exchanges of cash flows under the swap agreement will be

*Swap Exchanges*

|  | Echo | | Bank | |
| --- | --- | --- | --- | --- |
|  | Receive | Pay | Receive | Pay |
|  | £ | $ | $ | £ |
| Year 1 (interest) | 2,000,000 | 1,500,000 | 1,500,000 | 2,000,000 |
| Year 2 (interest) | 2,000,000 | 1,500,000 | 1,500,000 | 2,000,000 |
| Year 2 (principal) | 20,000,000 | 30,000,000 | 30,000,000 | 20,000,000 |
|  | 24,000,000 | 33,000,000 | 33,000,000 | 24,000,000 |

By the arrangement illustrated here, Echo has fixed a rate for exchanging the $30 million it will receive at the end of Year 2 by swapping $30 million in exchange for £20 million at the far-value date.

The investment potential of the cash flows exchanged at the end of Year 1 have been ignored in the table, and so the effective exchange rate that Echo has achieved is not apparent from the illustration. (If the interest rate on sterling remains at 10% and on the dollar it stays at 5%, the company would earn £200,000 in interest between the end of Year 1 and the end of Year 2, on the £2 million receivable at the end of Year 1. On the other hand, there would be an opportunity loss of 5% or $75,000 on the $1,500,000 payable at the end of Year 1. Taking these amounts of interest into the equation, the effective exchange rate for the swap is $1.3667 ($33.075 million ÷ £24.2 million). This is the rate that would, in principle, have been obtainable on a two year forward contract maturing at the end of the swap term.)

Echo also has an exposure for the interest payments of $1,500,000 in Year 1 and a further $1,500,000 in Year 2. It would probably avoid these exposures in practise by negotiating the swaps cash flows differently, or by other short-term hedging measures over the term of the swap. However, the concept that a swap can provide a long-term hedge for a transaction exposure is still evident from the example.

# Hedging and Speculation

The financial markets can be used to speculate rather than to hedge exposures with the aim of earning profits from risk-taking. Speculation is the opposite of hedging. It involves trading in established markets on the basis of informed judgments about how market prices will change. A speculator has the intention of making a profit from favorable exchange rate movements but could lose if exchange rates move the other way.

Speculation is a form of short-term investment activity. Foreign exchange speculators buy currencies with the intention of re-selling them at a profit in the near future, or sell currencies with the intention of buying them back at a profit. Large returns can be made on a fairly small investment within a short period of time.

This chapter focuses on currency speculation by non-bank corporates, although speculative positions also are taken by banks. For non-banks, however, speculative currency dealing should be either

- low risk, or
- contained, so that there is a maximum acceptable loss.

# Low Risk Speculation

Some speculation might be judged low risk and worthwhile, because the company is reasonably confident about the direction of future movements in a particular exchange rate. For example, a company with an exposure to pay Japanese yen at a future date would not be concerned about hedging that exposure if it believed that the yen would decline in value. The company would buy the yen when it was needed or when it felt that no further decline in value was likely. As a result the cost of buying the yen would be less than if it had hedged.

*Example*

Suppose that there is a large interest rate differential between the dollar (low interest) and sterling (high interest). A UK company might borrow $24 million for 12 months at 6% when the exchange rate was £1 = $1.50. It could then convert the dollars into £16 million and invest this for one year at, for example, 10%.

*Analysis*

The company would be hoping to profit from the interest rate differential between dollar borrowings and sterling investments. At 10% interest, the sterling investment will increase from £16 million to £17.6 million after one year. The dollar loan with interest must be repaid, at a cost of $25.44 million ($24 million x 1.06). If the exchange rate is above 1.445 ($25.44 million ÷ £17.6 million), the company will make a profit on its financial activities. For example, if the exchange rate after one year were still 1.50, it would cost the company £16.96 million ($25.44 million at 1.50) to repay the loan with interest, leaving it with a net profit of £0.64 million.

The speculative risk is that the exchange rate drops below £1 = $1.445 by the end of the 12-month period. If the company, although UK-based, had a regular income stream in dollars, this risk would be lessened by its ability to repay the dollar loan out of dollar earnings, because there would be no need to reconvert sterling into dollars at the end of the loan period. For UK companies with large earnings in dollars, the existence of a large interest rate differential between the dollar and sterling has at times provided an opportunity for very low-risk profit making.

# Higher Risk Speculation

On rare occasions, a company's treasury department (with board permission) speculates in the currency markets. Speculative transactions often will involve trades in derivative products. Any pure speculation of this kind by non-bank corporates is really a quasi-banking activity to earn profits from financial dealings, and it would not support the main commercial activities of the company (nor hedge commercial exposures). A danger of speculation is that if such transactions result in losses, they could be very heavy. Speculation should not be used as a substitute for earning profit from commercial activities and should be kept within the limits of what the company can afford.

A company could speculate on future movements in a spot rate by arranging forward exchange contracts.

For example, if a company expects the dollar to fall substantially against sterling in the next few months, it could arrange to

- sell dollars forward at today's forward prices, and
- buy dollars spot when the forward contract falls due for delivery, at a weaker spot rate.

The value date for the forward and spot transactions would be made to coincide, so that the speculator would earn an immediate cash profit.

If the dollar were expected to rise substantially in value, speculation might involve buying dollars forward and later selling them spot when the price had risen. Again, the value date for the forward and spot contracts would be made to coincide so there would be an immediate cash profit.

Speculation is easier for large companies with direct access to FX markets. They can get smaller spreads between bid and offer rates and so do not rely on substantial exchange rate movements to earn a speculator's profit. A large company also can bear a loss much more easily than a smaller one – speculation is always a gamble, irrespective of a company's confidence in its ability to forecast exchange rates.

There are two main dangers from currency speculation.

- The lure of easy profits in speculative activity can lead a dealer or corporate treasurer to take excessive risks to repeat the profit. Senior management, not fully understanding the risks, might encourage further speculation.

- Losses can be chased by doubling up positions in the expectation that the hoped-for changes in currency values will still happen. This is the classic reaction of a bad trader and is like a roulette gambler who, having lost $100 by betting on red, puts $200 on red the next time to make up the previous loss, and then having lost again, puts $400 on red yet another time, and so on, until the losses become huge.

*Case History 1*

Some years ago, a UK company announced that it had lost £147 million on foreign exchange dealings. Although the company did not specify the details, newspaper reports suggested that the losses resulted from speculative currency transactions. The company had anticipated that the dollar would continue to decline and was caught out by a sharp reversal in this trend and a sudden strengthening of the dollar.

The positions that the company took apparently involved two strategies

- Writing call options on the dollar. It is unusual for companies to write options, but the treasury departments in the big league sometimes do, although in most companies they are covered by underlying flows of currency from commercial activities. In this case, the scale of activity apparently exceeded the value of the company's dollar receivables by a substantial amount. Writing call options on the dollar at, for example, £1 = $1.80 would earn the company income from the premiums, and if the dollar fell in value (rose above 1.80), the options would not be exercised and the company would make a profit. However, if the dollar went up in value so that the exchange rate fell to below 1.80, the options would be exercised by their holders. The company apparently had had to buy dollars spot to meet its obligations when options were exercised, and in doing so made heavy losses.

- Selling dollars short against sterling in the foreign exchange markets by arranging forward contracts to sell dollars that the company did not have. Selling dollars short in the cash market would be profitable if the dollar fell in value. The idea is to fix a forward rate for selling dollars on date X, and as date X approaches, buy dollars at the current spot rate, and make a profit on the difference between buying and selling rates. Arranging forward contracts to sell dollars at 1.60 for example, would earn a speculative profit if the dollar spot rate weakens (goes above 1.60).

If the dollar had fallen in value against sterling, both of these strategies would have been profitable. However, because the dollar went up in value, its losses were substantial.

*Case History 2*
Some years ago, a multinational oil company reported a loss of several hundred million pounds arising out of unauthorized currency dealings by a Japanese associate company that had speculated unsuccessfully in dollar futures contracts.

The two case histories above raised a debate at the time about the role of the treasury department within large companies and whether they should be established as

- cost centers – i.e. departments that are accountable for the costs they incur, or
- profit centers – i.e. departments that should seek to make a profit on their activities by, where appropriate, charging other departments for the financial services they provide, in much the same way as an external bank.

There is a risk that treasury departments established as profit centers, unless properly controlled, could indulge in speculative trading and expose the organization to the risk of heavy losses.

# Comparing Hedging Methods

This book has tried to show how a company should make a policy decision about whether or not to hedge its currency exposures. Having made this decision, the aim of financial risk management is to select an appropriate mix of hedging methods to meet the policy requirements.

The key issues for a company's financial management to consider are

- What are the company's currency exposures?
- How significant are they?
- Should they be hedged?
- How should they be hedged?
- How successful has hedging been and what lessons can be learned?

# The Significance of Exposures

Currency risk is a function of exchange rate volatility. Within the euro zone, companies are now protected by the single currency for trading between countries in the zone. However, exchange rates between the major trading currencies (dollar, euro, yen, sterling etc.) have been volatile. Management of non-financial companies has woken up to the significance of currency risk management. In many industries, participants have a significant exposure to just a few major currencies.

*Deciding Whether to Hedge*
Risk is unavoidable. It is essential, however, to prevent exposures to risk

from becoming excessive, and a company should be able to absorb whatever losses might occur from unhedged risks. Keeping risk under control calls for a continuous monitoring process. Exposures should not arise without being noticed.

It should be recognized also that hedging can prevent a company from making windfall gains from favorable exchange rate movements. Although hedging exposures can deprive a company of large exchange gains, it should be recognized that hedging provides insurance against adverse events. Insurance can be expensive, but essential.

# Deciding How to Hedge

Transaction-based hedging techniques cannot protect a company against a permanent shift in an exchange rate, and are therefore inadequate for hedging long-term economic exposures.

As explained in previous chapters, hedging economic exposures calls for strategic decisions about

- shifting production facilities
- switching to a different market
- changing purchasing policy for key materials or components.

In some global industries such as car production, manufacturers have spread production facilities, opening plants in different countries in an attempt to avoid trade barriers and to reduce exposures to currency fluctuations. If necessary, production and sourcing can be switched from one country to another in response to any permanent shift in exchange rates.

Short-term exposures can be hedged selectively. Companies generally are reluctant to admit that they indulge in currency speculation, but it is probably common practise to hedge selectively

- taking action to hedge exposures where an adverse exchange rate movement could occur, but

- remaining exposed to currencies when a favorable exchange rate movement is anticipated.

Companies are likely to choose a mixture of hedging techniques for transaction exposures. The basic mix will consist of

- structural hedging (netting receipts and expenditures in the same currency)
- accepting some risk between currencies whose exchange rate is expected to remain stable, for example, the dollar/Hong Kong dollar rate)
- shifting the risk to the customer or supplier by insisting on sales or purchases in domestic currency
- external hedging techniques, particularly forward exchange contracts.

*Outright Hedging and Options*
A distinction can be made between

- outright hedging techniques that effectively lock in an exchange rate for a transaction (forward contracts, swaps, futures), and
- options.

Outright hedging costs less to obtain, e.g. there is no transaction cost for arranging a forward contract, but involves a binding contract. If the underlying transaction fails to materialize and the expected cash flow does not occur, a currency exposure arises from the hedging instrument itself. Options, although costly to purchase, do not have this risk.

Individual financial managers have their own preferences for hedging instruments, although exchange-traded instruments (futures and traded options) and swaps will be more relevant to larger companies and banks.

The table opposite provides a useful comparison between forward exchange contracts, currency futures, borrowing and options.

# Hedging Instruments Compared

| | Forward contract | Currency borrowing | Currency options | Currency futures |
|---|---|---|---|---|
| Want to hedge a specific transaction | ◆ | ◆ | ◆ | ◆ |
| Simplicity of arrangements and monitoring | ◆ | | | |
| Want opportunity to profit from favorable exchange rate movements | | | ◆ | |
| Need for flexibility | | ◆ | ◆ | |
| Uncertainty about amount of currency, whether the exposure will exist or timing of exposure | | ◆ | ◆ | |
| Need to keep credit lines with banks unaffected | | | ◆ | ◆ |
| Want a comparatively cheap short-term hedge | ◆ | | ◆ | ◆ |
| Exposure period | Mostly short term, can be over 1 year | Short or long term | Short term | Short term |
| Comment | Use only if matching not possible. Most commonly used hedging instrument | Variable interest rates make interest cost/income uncertain | Use only if perceived advantage of potential currency gain outweighs the cost | Not often used for hedging currency exposures |

# Accounting Implications

Currency hedging has implications for a company's profit and loss account and balance sheet. There are several general rules for accounting that ought to be followed.

- A coherent and consistent accounting policy should be defined at the outset. This policy should ensure that the accounting for a transaction reflects economic reality and applies fundamental accounting principles and concepts.
- The policy should be explained to the financial managers of each business unit and approved by the company's auditors.
- The policy should be adhered to unless circumstances change requiring a revision. Accounting policy should not be altered regularly in order to improve the reported profits for the year. Any revision of policy must be cleared with the company's auditors.

If these rules are adopted, the year-end accounting work will be minimized and the possibility of a challenge to the company's taxable profits from the tax authorities will be reduced because the company will point to a coherent and consistent approach over a number of years.

This chapter aims to provide an overview of the accounting issues involved in accounting for foreign currency items.

There are several aspects to accounting for foreign currency items. They include

- recording gains or losses on currency transactions
- recording gains or losses on currency translation

- measuring gains or losses on instruments used for currency hedging.

Accounting for gains or losses on currency transactions and translation is relatively straightforward.

However, accounting standards on financial instruments that are used to hedge currency exposures are still at an early stage of development. Measurement standards exist in some countries. In particular, there are detailed measurement rules in the US (Statement 133) and there is also an International Accounting Standard (IAS 39: Financial Instruments, Recognition and Measurement).

The actual rules applied by a company will depend on the jurisdiction in question, and will not be explained in detail here. For example, Statement 133 in the US is highly complex with a huge number of exceptions, thus making it difficult to apply general principles to accounting practise.

# Structural Hedging: Exchange Gains and Losses

Structural hedging of receipts and payments reduces or eliminates currency exposure, and avoids cash losses from unfavorable exchange rate movements. This should be reflected in a company's accounting records.

*Example*
A UK company sells goods to a customer abroad for $800,000 on November 1, with payment due on February 1. It also buys goods from abroad for $800,000 on December 1, with payment due on February 1.

| Exchange rates: | £1 = |
| --- | --- |
| November 1 | $1.40 |
| December 1 | $1.45 |
| February 1 | $1.43 |

The company decides to match the dollar receipt on February 1 with the dollar payment due on the same date.

The accounting records of the company will be

|  |  | £ |
|---|---|---|
| On November 1 | Sales (÷ 1.40) | 571,429 |
|  | Debtor (÷ 1.40) | 571,429 |
| On December 1 | Purchases (÷ 1.45) | 551,724 |
|  | Creditor (÷ 1.45) | 551,724 |

On February 1, the $800,000 received will be used to pay the supplier. In the accounts, the settlement of the debtor and the creditor will be recorded at the spot rate of 1.43.

|  | Debtor | Creditor |
|---|---|---|
|  | £ | £ |
| Amount receivable/payable (£ equivalent) | 571,429 | 551,724 |
| Value of payment | (÷ 1.43) 559,441 | (÷ 1.43) 559,441 |
| Loss on exchange | 11,988 | 7,717 |

The total loss on exchange is £19,705.

In the accounts, this exchange loss occurs because the company had an exposure of $800,000 of income in the period November 1 to December 1 when the expected income was matched against the expected payments. Because of the exchange rate movement in that period, the sale of $800,000 was recorded as £571,429 and the purchase of $800,000 was recorded as only £551,724. If you think of sales minus purchases as profit, the company earned a profit of £19,705 (£571,429 - £551,724). The exchange loss of £19,705 on February 1 simply offsets this profit, leaving neither profit nor loss from the exchange rate movements.

# Forward Exchange Contracts

Differing accounting procedures might be adopted for forward contracts, according to why the forward contract was taken out. Here we shall look at a situation where a company arranges a forward contract as a hedge for a specific foreign currency transaction. There are two basic issues to consider.

- Should the forward contract be linked to the transaction for which it is a hedge, or should the transaction and the forward contract be accounted for separately?
- Should the premium or discount for the forward contract exchange rate (compared to the spot rate) be treated as a finance charge/income, or not? The premium or discount (the forward adjustment) represents the value of the interest rate differential between the two currencies.

*Example*
A UK company purchases goods from the US costing $648,000.

Purchase date     November 1, Year 1

Payment date     February 1, Year 2

| Date | Spot rate | 3-month forward |
|------|-----------|-----------------|
| November 1, Year 1 | 1.50 | 1.48 |
| December 31, Year 1 | 1.47 | |
| February 1, Year 2 | 1.44 | |

The company hedges the currency exposure on November 1 by taking out a three month forward contract to buy $648,000 at £1 = $1.48. The company's accounting year ends on December 31.

*Analysis*
There are two ways of accounting for this transaction.

*Method 1*

Record the $648,000 purchase transaction and the creditor at the forward (contracted) rate.

|  |  | Debit | Credit |
|---|---|---|---|
| Purchases | (÷ 1.48) | £437,838 | |
| Creditor | (÷ 1.48) | | £437,838 |

There will be no gain or loss on exchange.

*Method 2*

The purchase transaction and the forward contract are treated as separate transactions. The premium/discount (forward adjustment) is also treated separately, as an interest charge or income item. In this example there is a forward adjustment of 2 cents (1.50 - 1.48) between the spot rate at the time of the forward transaction and the forward rate obtained.

Method 2 is suggested in the US by FASB 52 but method 1 is permitted in the UK by SSAP 20. Method 1 is simpler. Under Method 2, the accounting entries would be

At November 1

|  |  | Debit | Credit |
|---|---|---|---|
| Purchases | (spot rate 1.50) | £432,000 | |
| Creditor | (spot rate 1.50) | | £432,000 |

The company's year-end is December 31, and the creditor should be revalued at the year-end rate to £440,816 ($648,000 ÷ 1.47). There is a loss on exchange of £8,816, (£440,816 - £432,000) from the creditor revaluation. This will be written off to the income statement for the year.

At the same time, there is an exchange gain on the forward contract of £8,816.

|  | £ |
|---|---|
| $648,000 at spot rate of 1.50, November 1: | |
| contracted amount payable | 432,000 |
| $648,000 at closing rate of 1.47, December 31: | |
| amount payable at current value | 440,816 |
| Gain on exchange | 8,816 |

The exchange gain and the exchange loss of £8,816 are self-canceling.

The forward contract to buy dollars locked in a more expensive dollar price than the spot rate on the contract transaction date (November 1), and the forward contract therefore has an interest cost.

|  | £ |
|---|---|
| $648,000 at spot rate of 1.50 | 432,000 |
| $640,000 at forward rate of 1.48 | 437,838 |
| Interest cost of premium | 5,838 |

This cost is treated as an interest charge that can be time-apportioned between accounting periods as follows

|  | £ |
|---|---|
| The two months from November 1, Year 1 to the end of Year 1 (2/3) | 3,892 |
| The one month from January 1 to February 1, Year 2 (1/3) | 1,946 |
|  | 5,838 |

At February 1

|  | Debit | Credit |
|---|---|---|
|  | £ | £ |
| Creditor paid (end of Year 1 valuation) | 440,816 | |
| Interest charge paid | 5,838 | |
| Cash payment (forward contract) | | 437,838 |
| Gain on exchange account, balance now written off | | 8,816 |
|  | 446,654 | 446,654 |

The key features of Method 2 are that

- the original transaction is recorded in the accounts at the spot rate, not the forward rate
- gains or losses on the debtor or creditor will be offset by equal losses or gains on the forward contract
- the forward adjustment is accounted for as a finance cost or as interest income, depending on whether the forward rate obtained is less or more favorable than the spot rate at the time of the forward transaction.

# Currency Swaps

Currency swaps will be accounted for in the same way as forward contracts. A company entering into a currency swap in order to hedge foreign currency borrowings is likely to translate the borrowing in its balance sheet at the swap rate, i.e. take account of the commercial effect of the swap.

# Currency Futures

The initial margin (cash deposit) that must be paid for a futures contract is repayable when the contract matures or is sold. Therefore in the balance sheet, an initial margin will be included among current assets because it is collateral that has been put on deposit.

Variation margins are different because they represent gains or losses on futures trading. These gains or losses might be

- reflected in the profit and loss account as they occur, for example, if the futures were purchased for speculative purposes, or to hedge longer-term foreign currency assets or liabilities, or

- deferred, and released to the profit and loss account to match the income or expenditure of currency that the futures contract is intended to hedge.

Under both international and US standards various criteria must be satisfied before hedging treatment is allowed.

When the initial margin (refundable cash deposit) is paid, the accounting entry will be

CREDIT    Cash

DEBIT     Initial margin account (current asset)

When this is eventually repaid, the accounting entry is simply reversed.

When variation margins are paid as a result of losses, the accounting entries are

CREDIT    Cash

DEBIT     Variation margin account

Subsequently:

CREDIT    Variation margin account

DEBIT     either a) Income statement (Profit and loss account)

          or     b) Deferred loss on hedge account

If a company's futures position shows a profit, it can be recorded in the variation margin account.

DEBIT     Variation margin account

CREDIT    Deferred gain on hedge account

Subsequently:

DEBIT     Cash (when the cash is received)

CREDIT    Variation margin account

DEBIT     Deferred gain or hedge account

CREDIT    Profit and loss account

# Currency Options

There is no official guidance on how to account for currency options, but there are several reasons why options can't be accounted for in the same way as forward exchange contracts.

- An option might never be exercised, even when it is being used to hedge specific transaction exposures.
- The strike price might not be the spot exchange rate when the option is purchased.
- An option costs money to buy, and an option buyer must pay a premium. The size of the premium represents the value of the option at the time the option is written. There must be an accounting treatment for the option premium.

As a general rule, accounting for options should reflect the hedge on the underlying transaction.

Options can be used as a hedge in the following ways.

*Situation 1.* A company contracts to buy or sell goods abroad. A future delivery date is fixed, and the customer agrees to pay cash on delivery. If the sale price is in the exporter's currency, the customer purchases a call option, for expiry on the delivery/payment date. If the sale price is in the customer's currency, the exporter purchases a put option.

*Situation 2.* A company buys or sells goods abroad on credit, with the payment date at some time in the future. Either the company or the customer purchases an option now, to expire on payment date at the end of the credit period.

The difference between the two situations is that in the first there will be no underlying trade debtor or creditor in the accounts, because the sale will not be made until delivery. This makes accounting for the option easier. In Situation 2, there is an underlying trade debtor or creditor in the accounts, because delivery of the goods has taken place, and this complicates the problem of accounting.

*No Underlying Debtor or Creditor*

Let's begin with the simpler situation, where an option is purchased to hedge a future currency payment or receipt, but there is no underlying creditor or debtor in the accounts. The option is purchased to hedge a future payment or receipt where cash will be paid immediately on delivery of the goods. There are three ways of accounting for the option premium in these circumstances.

*Method 1*

Write off the cost of the premium at the time of purchasing the currency option. The premium cost therefore will be charged in full, as a finance charge, to the accounting period in which the option is purchased.

*Method 2*

Record the cost of the premium as an asset. Retain this asset in the balance sheet at cost until the option expires or is exercised.

On expiry or exercise, write off the cost of this premium to the profit and loss account as a finance charge. The premium cost therefore will be charged in full to the accounting period in which the option expires or is exercised.

*Method 3*

Record the cost of the premium as an asset and then amortize this cost over the life of the asset as a finance charge in the profit and loss account.

All three methods will give the same overall end result, and they differ only when the option has not expired or been exercised at the accounting year end. In this circumstance, the three methods will allocate the cost of the option differently between one accounting year and the next, and give a different balance sheet valuation for the option premium.

In the balance sheet, the premium's value will be

*Method 1* - nil

*Method 2* - at its original cost

*Method 3* - at its amortized cost

Auditors will accept any of these three treatments provided that the policy is explained to them at the outset and adhered to consistently. This will ensure that the accounting policy for options is not altered in order to manipulate the profit figure in any given year.

### Underlying Debtor or Creditor

When an option is used to hedge the payment from an existing creditor or to an existing debtor, there is likely to be an exchange gain or loss on the creditor or debtor. There ought to be an offsetting exchange loss or gain on the option because this is the reason for hedging.

The accounting procedures might be

Record the debtor or creditor at the spot rate as at the date of the transaction.

Record the option premium initially at cost as an asset. Write off this cost by one of three methods

- in full at the time of purchase
- in full on expiry
- by amortizing over the option's life.

There may be a gain or loss on exchange when the payment is eventually made equal to the difference between the balance sheet value of the debtor or creditor and the actual cash received or paid. If this difference shows a gain on the option, the option premium should be revalued upwards by the amount of this difference, minus any option premium cost written off or amortized. The revaluation is a gain on exchange in the income statement. If this difference shows a loss on the option, the option should be revalued downwards by the amount of the loss. If this loss exceeds the cost of the premium, the premium should be written off in full.

*Example*

A UK company has bought goods abroad costing $1,500,000. The exchange rate at the date of the transaction (June 30) was £1 = $1.50, and payment is due in three months, on September 30.

The company decides to hedge this exposure by buying options to sell £1,000,000 in exchange for dollars at £1 = $1.50, with an expiry date of September 30. The premium paid is £30,000. It is company policy to write off the cost of the premium in full on the date of purchase.

**Exchange rate: £1 =**

At August 31      1.40

At September 30  1.35

*Analysis*

On June 30, the purchase on credit will be recorded in the accounts at the spot rate of 1.50 (£1,000,000).

| DEBIT | Purchases | £1,000,000 |
|---|---|---|
| CREDIT | Creditors account | £1,000,000 |

The cost of the premium will be recorded in an asset account.

| DEBIT | Option premium (asset account) | £30,000 |
|---|---|---|
| CREDIT | Cash | £30,000 |

On September 30, when the option expires in-the-money, it will be exercised, with £1,000,000 sold in exchange for $1,500,000, and the dollars used to pay the creditor.

| | £ | |
|---|---|---|
| At June 30, creditor | 1,000,000 | exposure hedged |
| Cash paid, September 30 | (1,000,000) | |
| Gain/loss on exchange | 0 | |

The option premium of £30,000 will be written off as a charge in the profit and loss account.

CREDIT    Option premium £30,000
DEBIT     Profit and loss account £30,000

# Taxation Aspects

Companies also need to be aware of the taxation aspects of hedging currency exposures. What might seem a suitable method for hedging an exposure before allowing for taxation could become much less suitable when the taxation costs are considered. Tax rules vary from one country to another.

*Caution*
- Tax law and practise varies from country to country; consequently a multinational company should know about taxation in every country where it has subsidiaries or branch operations.
- Tax law can change over time.

# US Stock Markets

# Introduction

The US stock markets trade securities of both US corporations and some non-US companies.

US investors can buy shares in non-US companies in markets outside the US: however, a larger potential investor market exists for non-US companies that can offer their shares in the US markets. They can do this by

- issuing registered shares on a recognised stock market, such as the New York Stock Exchange, or
- issuing unregistered securities in the private placement market under Rule 144A that is described later.

With the exception of some Canadian companies, most non-US companies issue shares in the US in the form of American Depository Receipts or ADRs. In most cases, one ADR represents a larger quantity of the company's underlying shares.

There are a large number of stock markets in the US, ranging from the major national stock markets to smaller regional stock exchanges and self-regulated networks of securities dealers using an electronic screen-based over-the-counter (OTC) trading system.

Over-the-counter trading, in its original sense, means trading in shares that are not listed on a stock exchange. However, the meaning of over-the-counter has developed, and the term is often used to mean trading that takes place by telephone.

The most important screen-based OTC system is Nasdaq, the National Association of Securities Dealers Automatic Quotations System.

The three largest stock markets in the US are

- The New York Stock Exchange
- Nasdaq
- American Stock Exchange

*The Third Market*

In the US, when shares are listed on a stock exchange, by no means all trading in those shares goes through the exchange. This is in contrast to the UK for example, where most trading in listed shares goes through London Stock Exchange dealers.

The term third market refers to OTC trading in shares listed on an exchange. Dealers who are not members of the exchange can make a market in any listed shares they choose. (They are likely to choose heavily traded shares, for which demand is high.) Their clients are mainly investment institutions. In recent years, the US stock exchanges have lost a substantial volume of trading business to OTC rivals such as Instinet and the electronic communications networks (ECNs).

# The New York Stock Exchange

The New York Stock Exchange is the world's largest stock market. It is sometimes referred to by market participants as the Big Board. Trading in securities is centred on the floor of the exchange, and there is a specialist on the exchange floor for each individual stock listed on the exchange. However, the trading system is highly automated and provides immediate access for dealers across the country.

*How an order is processed*

The investing public places its orders, usually by telephone, through sales personnel of a brokerage house or stock brokers. Orders are then transmitted from the branch office of the brokerage house to the NYSE trading floor through an electronic communications and order-processing system.

Each stock listed on the NYSE is allocated to a broker known as a specialist. A specialist trades only in that stock, and at a specified location on the floor of the exchange called a trading post. The specialist provides the focal point for incoming buy and sell orders.

Buyers and sellers are represented on the exchange floor by floor brokers. The floor brokers meet openly at the relevant trading post to find the best price in the security. Bids to buy and offers to sell are made by open outcry. When the highest bid meets the lowest offer, a trade is executed. The NYSE system is an order driven system, using open outcry.

If the market is unable to match buyers and sellers, the specialist will buy stock for which there is no other buyer and will sell stock for which there is no other seller. The existence of specialists ensures that two-way prices are always available. Prices are reported to the exchange authorities and displayed, so that real-time price information is available to all participants in the market.

*SuperDOT*

The SuperDOT system is an electronic order-routing system through which member firms of the NYSE transmit orders directly to the trading post where the securities are traded. After the order has been executed in the auction market, a report of the transaction is returned to the member's office through the same communications circuit that brought the order to the trading floor. By means of the SuperDOT network, a member firm in, for example Los Angeles, can transmit an order on behalf of a client to the NYSE, and without any of the firm's personnel having to take any other action, the transaction can be executed and reported back less than 30 seconds later.

*Settlement and Clearing*

Settlement of transactions on the NYSE occurs on T+3.

There are a number of clearing system providers. These include

    The Midwest Clearing Corporation (MCC)
    The Depository Trust Company (DTC)

# Nasdaq and the American Stock Exchange

In 1998, Nasdaq merged with the American Stock Exchange to form the Nasdaq-Amex Market Group Inc. However, although they have the same holding company, Nasdaq and Amex operate as separate stock markets.

# Nasdaq

The Nasdaq Stock Market, established in 1971, was the world's first electronic screen-based stock market.

Essentially, it is an electronic price quotation system that allows its users to trade in securities at prices quoted by dealers on real-time price information screens. Dealers in the Nasdaq stock market quote competitive two-way prices – bid and offer prices – for the listed shares in which they deal. Price information is transmitted to terminals in dealing rooms and offices throughout the US and also in other countries. The simultaneous transmission of quotes and orders to all terminals worldwide allows all Nasdaq participants equal access to the market and to market information.

Transactions in shares are made by telephone rather than by electronic dealing system, between a dealer and a customer at the price currently quoted by the dealer.

Orders also can be initiated on-line through the internet. In such cases, the investor uses an on-line trading account and places the order electronically with an on-line brokerage. The trade is then executed by the broker or an electronic communications network (ECN) at the current best available market price.

*Nasdaq International*
Nasdaq introduced a transatlantic, international service in 1992, providing a screen-based price quotation system designed to operate across time zones. The system operates in London between 08.30 and 14.00 (London time) on each US business day. This allows dealers in London to trade either in the US or the UK at any time between the start of the trading day in London and the close of the US markets. Securities qualifying for a quotation on Nasdaq International include

- securities of US companies listed on Nasdaq
- equity securities listed on any US securities exchange
- securities of foreign companies (except for Canadian companies) listed on Nasdaq
- American Depository Receipts (ADRs) listed on Nasdaq.

# The American Stock Exchange

The American Stock Exchange (Amex) is the second-largest floor-based securities exchange in the US. It trades both listed securities and derivatives. It is located in New York.

The Amex is an auction market in which prices are determined by public orders to buy and sell. The auction market procedures ensure that public buyers and sellers obtain the best available prices by centralising order flow and requiring market professionals to yield priority to public investors.

# Regulation in the US

The Securities and Exchange Commission (SEC) is the regulatory body for the US securities industry. Futures and options markets are regulated by the Commodity and Futures Trading Commission or CFTC. Banking in the US is regulated by the Federal Reserve Board.

*The Securities Act 1933: registering securities*
The Securities Act 1933 was introduced after the Wall Street Crash of 1929 to protect investors. It requires companies to make a detailed registration with the SEC before any of its securities can be offered for sale to the public.

A condition of registration is the preparation of a prospectus for the issue that must be made available to all potential investors. The prospectus must contain detailed information about the nature of the issuer's business and the reasons for the issue, together with detailed financial information about the issuer.

The registration process is lengthy, particularly for non-US companies seeking a listing on a US exchange, but all shares to be offered for sale to the public must be registered.

Unregistered shares may be offered to institutional investors, however, via the private placement market.

*Private placement market*
Section 144 of the Securities Act 1933 permits the issue of unregistered securities and secondary market trading in unregistered securities, but only in cases where the buyers of the securities are investors with capital markets experience and large financial resources, i.e. mainly institutional investors.

Unregistered US securities can be issued and sold to experienced investors by means of private placement, i.e. by targeted selling of the issue to institutional investors. Secondary market trading can then take place over the counter.

The main advantage of the private placement market is that although there are restrictions on potential investors, equities or debt securities can be issued without the delays and expense of registration with the SEC.

Until 1990, the private placement market was not accessible to non-US companies. This situation changed with the introduction of Rule 144A.

*Rule 144A*

In 1990, the rules regarding the private placement market were modified by the introduction of Rule 144A to the Securities Act. The purpose of the new rule was to create a bigger and more liquid private placement market. This allows non-US companies to issue shares on the US private placement market. Such shares must not be of the same class as any shares listed on a US stock exchange, i.e. must not be fungible with any listed shares in the US. However, shares can be listed on a foreign stock exchange.

# Instinet

Instinet claims to be the world's largest agency brokerage. Created by Reuters, it provides a range of equity trading and research services.

In its trading operations, Instinet provides block trading, order management and crossing services in global equities. It has evolved so that, regardless of market structure or regulatory regime, it can provide agency trading services for its clients. It is a member of various stock exchanges in the Americas, Europe and Asia, and trades in many markets around the world.

Instinet's edge comes from its success in focusing on reduced transaction costs. Its aim is the same as that of any other institutional trading firm — to secure as many institutional orders as possible and execute them at the best prices possible, anywhere in the world.

Instinet's trading strategy is the same as other firms that manage institutional orders during market hours. This strategy is to represent pieces of an institutional client's order simultaneously in as many different pools of liquidity as possible. For example, if handling a client order for shares in French company Elf Acquitaine, pieces of this order would be represented simultaneously on the Paris market (CAC), SEAQ International in London and the New York Stock Exchange.

Instinet attempts to match buyers and sellers of lines of stock. Any member firm with access to the system can input an order to buy or sell at a certain price and up to a certain expiry time. The order will be transmitted throughout the market to try to find someone willing to provide the other side of the trade. This could be a broker, market maker or institution. If the other side is found, a bargain is struck, and the trade is reported to the relevant exchange authorities in the normal way.

# Electronic Communications Networks (ECNs)

ECNs are computerised trade-matching systems, that match best bid and offer prices. At the same time they provide trade anonymity to users and also cut trading costs by by-passing broker-dealer commissions and exchange fees (charges to investors for access to price quotations).

Computer-based trading systems also offer the possibility of after-market-hours trading.

ECNs automate the trading process. Many market professionals believe that stock exchanges of the future will be based on the ECN model. In 1997, the SEC established a regulatory platform for ECN capabilities in the US market place. In 1998, the SEC passed regulations permitting the creation of all-electronic stock exchanges.

There are over a dozen ECNs operating in the US but this number will probably rise fairly quickly.

### The major ECNs

Instinet, as well as seeing itself as the world's largest agency broker, also considers itself as an ECN, trading a large proportion of total volumes on Nasdaq. It is unlikely to seek status as a stock exchange.

In 1999, Instinet and on-line retail broker E*Trade announced an agreement to provide after-hours on-line trading to retail clients. Under this arrangement, Instinet offers after-hours trading (16.00 to 18.30 UK time) to both institutional and retail customers in Nasdaq and NYSE stocks. This arrangement marked the first time that retail investors were offered access to Instinet.

Other major ECNs include

### Island.

This specialises in retail market trades including day trading, and handles a significant proportion (about 10%) of Nasdaq trading volume.

### REDIBook

### Tradebook SuperECN

### Archipelago

Archipelago offers a best-execution model: orders are allowed to go off the system if a better price exists elsewhere on another ECN. This differs from other ECNs that provide a centralised book and limit trading to orders on the book, i.e. limit trading to the system's own liquidity. The Archipelago model of connecting to all the other ECNs and allowing access to them is probably more attractive to investors than stand alone ECNs.

# International Stock Markets and Trading Systems

There are many domestic equity markets around the world, varying in size and liquidity. Investors have a wide choice of countries or regions in which to invest.

Thanks to modern communications and dealing systems, investors are able to invest in foreign equities by purchasing the shares directly in the domestic stock market of the companies concerned.

There are two types of trading system:

- quote-driven systems
- order-driven systems.

The London Stock Exchange uses both types of system.

A *quote-driven system* is one in which share prices are quoted, for example by market makers on a screen, and share transactions are made with a market maker at or around the price the market maker is quoting. In return for making continuous prices and agreeing to deal with other market participants, market makers are rewarded by being allowed to make a profit or turn on the spread, i.e. the difference between the buying and selling prices of the shares.

For example, a market maker in shares of XYZ plc might quote prices of 500 – 505, meaning that it will buy shares in XYZ at 500p and sell them at 505p. The 5p difference is the market maker's spread.

An *order-driven system* is one in which the existence of buy or sell orders for shares in a company determines the prices at which transactions in those shares are made. There is no spread. Buy and sell orders are matched at the same price, normally automatically by the electronic trading system. The prices that would-be buyers and sellers input to the system must be compatible, otherwise a trade is impossible.

Although order-driven systems are nowadays mainly electronic systems, another form of order-driven system is open outcry that is still used in some exchanges, particularly in derivatives exchanges in the US. Open outcry involves a group of market participants operating on the trading floor of an exchange and executing incoming buy and sell orders by shouting or signalling their orders, and finding another trader who is willing to act as counterparty in the transaction.

Most *institutional business* in shares in the US and the UK is now transacted off screen or off market and at different prices from those shown on screens. This is because many transactions by institutional investors (pension funds, etc.) are so large that they need to be the subject of individual negotiation between the institution (or the institution's representative) and the market participant trading the stock.

# Introduction of SETS (1997)

In 1997, the London Stock Exchange replaced the quote-driven SEAQ system for trading shares in the top 100 stocks with an automated order book – an order-driven system called the Stock Exchange Electronic Trading System or SETS.

When using SETS, investors place orders through a stock exchange member firm for inclusion in the electronic order book. Orders remain on the order book until a counterparty is found at the desired price, or until the order is deleted, or until the order reaches its expiry time or date when it is removed from the order book without having been transacted. Once they are on the order book, orders are transacted automatically.

Only member firms of the Stock Exchange or SETS Participants may input orders or execute against existing orders on the order book. Non-members cannot access the order book directly, and must use a member firm or SETS Participant as intermediary to carry out trades.

# The SETS Order Book

The order book is used for shares in the UK's largest companies, i.e. the companies making up the FTSE 100, plus FTSE 100 reserve stocks, stocks in the Eurotop 300 Index and shares for which options are traded on LIFFE. In addition, if a company moves out of the FTSE 100, its shares will continue to be traded on the SETS order book.

The SETS order book is based on an order matching system in which member firms display their bid (buying) and offer (selling) orders to the market on an electronic order book. The book is open from 08.00 hrs to 16.30, Monday to Friday (except public holidays). The order book is therefore a list of bid and offer orders waiting to be transacted. However, very large orders are often transacted off the order book, for example by telephone.

Details of all orders are held centrally by the Stock Exchange. Participants add orders or execute against existing orders by sending electronic messages to the system. Executions occur automatically in accordance with strict price and time priority, so that investors can be confident that their orders will be executed fairly.

# SEAQ

SEAQ (Stock Exchange Automated Quotation) is a continuously updated data base that distributes information about market makers' bid and offer prices to the market. Registered market makers must maintain quoted prices during the mandatory quote period (08.00 to 16.30, Monday to Friday). SEAQ can be viewed on a number of screen-based information services such as Reuters and Bloomberg.

SEAQ includes

- a price dissemination service, distributing market makers' quoted prices to the market
- a trade ticker that publishes details of all trades reported to SEAQ

● the market makers' bid and offer prices and trade sizes to which these prices relate that are used to create the SEAQ yellow strip.

The yellow strip, so called because of its colour on the SEAQ screen, identifies at any moment in the trading day, from an investor's point of view, the best available bid and offer prices (the touch) for every SEAQ security, and it also identifies (by code name) up to four market makers quoting this price. Other market makers' names and quotes also can be viewed on the screen.

# SEATS Plus

The Stock Exchange Alternative Trading Service (SEATS Plus) provides a combination of competing quotes and/or firm orders for companies' shares. SEATS Plus supports the trading of AIM stocks and shares in fully listed companies that do not have competing market makers for their shares, and so do not have the status to trade via SEAQ.

SEATS Plus provides an order board through which orders to buy and sell shares can be displayed and matched.

There is also a facility for competing price quotations, allowing one or more market makers to display quoted prices in a company's shares throughout the day.

# SEAQ International

SEAQ International is the London Stock Exchange's market display mechanism for international securities. Companies quoted on SEAQ International benefit from exposure to an international investment market, while investors benefit from a visible, regulated trading facility.

Usually share prices are quoted in the domestic currency of the company concerned, and transactions are settled through the local settlement system of the country. Trading in the international securities market operates 24 hours a day, but price quotations can be input to SEAQ International only between 07.30 and 17.15 UK time.

The market operates on a competing market maker quote-based system. Registered market makers are required to display bid and offer prices during the mandatory quote period (07.30 to 16.30) and the maximum bargain size to which these prices relate.

### techMARK

techMARK was the outcome in 1999 of an effort by the London Stock Exchange to stop losing business to rival stock exchanges such as Nasdaq and the Neuer Markt that are perceived to be more friendly to young high-tech companies. The LSE has described techMARK as a market within a market: it is a grouping together of growth technology companies from a wide range of industrial sectors into a market with its own FTSE Index.

In fact, techMARK is not much more than a stock market index, and in spite of small changes in the listing rules for the companies involved, all techMARK stocks are quoted, trade and settle in the same way as other LSE stocks. There is in effect no new market. However, proposed new listing rules for techMARK stocks will offer access to a LSE listing for a wider range of innovative growth companies. Consideration is being given to concessionary listings for companies that do not meet the traditional three-year trading record requirement for fully listed stocks.

Provided the company comes from a key industrial sub sector identified as a focus for techMARK, its shares will qualify automatically for involvement in the market. Other companies can be put forward for inclusion by their corporate broker or sponsor. Applications are considered by the exchange and an independent group of market experts.

# The Alternative Investment Market (AIM)

The Alternative Investment Market (AIM) was established by the LSE in 1995, specifically for small, young and growing companies. AIM has established a well-defined role as a source of equity finance for growing companies. Its rules are designed to reflect the nature of the companies on the market: for this reason, AIM companies are not bound by the full listing rules of the LSE. Instead they have their own rule book with less stringent requirements.

Each AIM company must have a nominated adviser. The nominated adviser in effect acts as broker to the initial AIM issue (bringing the company to the market) and supports the company on an ongoing basis thereafter. The nominated broker therefore takes on greater responsibility for the launched AIM company than is required from the sponsor of a fully listed company on the main market.

AIM is a Recognised Investment Exchange, operated by the London Stock Exchange. It ensures that the infrastructure is in place to regulate and operate the market efficiently, and it offers services to market users, including a secure and timely means of settling UK share transactions through CREST. Any type or class of security can be admitted to AIM but, in practise, most AIM securities are ordinary shares.

# Trading on AIM

The London Stock Exchange promotes the liquidity of shares in AIM companies through the use of the SEATS Plus system.

# Ofex

Ofex is an off-exchange share matching and trading facility, established in 1995, for companies that for one reason or another do not want to join the main market or AIM. Many of the stocks listed on Ofex are illiquid and often have large family shareholdings.

Price quotes are indicative only and in small sizes. Spreads are wider than for shares quoted on the main market and some stocks can go for months without being traded.

Ofex was established by J P Jenkins Limited to enable London Stock Exchange member firms to deal in the securities of unlisted and unquoted companies. Securities on Ofex are not deemed to be listed, quoted or dealt in on the London Stock Exchange, nor are they subject to any rules of the LSE.

J P Jenkins is the principal market maker in all Ofex-traded securities and makes a price in all such securities during the course of each trading day. It also processes applications from companies wishing to use an Ofex trading facility for their shares.

As the operator and principal market maker of Ofex, J P Jenkins undertakes to quote a firm two-way price (bid and offer prices) in a given quantity of stock for most Ofex securities. For illiquid securities, it will quote a basis price and seek to match an incoming trade with existing indicated business that previously has been notified to it. Ofex prices are posted in summary form in the *Financial Times* and are provided by a number of information vendors, such as Bloomberg and Reuters.

# Ofex and AIM Compared

In contrast to Ofex, AIM is regulated by the London Stock Exchange, and each AIM company requires the services of a nominated adviser and a nominated broker. Ofex, on the other hand, is technically not a market, even though it is referred to as a market by the press. Ofex is simply a dealing facility off-exchange, but operated by a Stock Exchange member firm (which in turn is regulated by the SFA).

# Tradepoint

The Tradepoint Stock Exchange is an electronic order-driven stock exchange. It was created for the benefit of fund managers, market makers and broker dealers. Set up in 1997, it is a Recognised Investment Exchange and is a competitor to the London Stock Exchange. (Tradepoint is a limited company whose shares are listed on AIM.)

An attraction of Tradepoint for users is that it is the only foreign stock exchange currently cleared to operate in the US for trading in US stocks. To gain this approval. Tradepoint has agreed with the US authorities to limit its daily volume in US shares to less than 10% of the volume handled by the London Stock Exchange. However, its direct access to the US market provides investors with a taste of what could become a viable alternative to the established US stock markets – a centralised, electronic, order-driven US exchange that is open to traditional members of the club as well as to mutual funds and on-line brokers.

To date, Tradepoint has not captured a significant share of the market for UK stocks.

# Germany

The German economy has been relatively poorly represented by its stock exchanges, with the market capitalisation of quoted German companies totalling a far smaller percentage of gross domestic product than in the US or the UK. This situation is the consequence of the historic role of German banks in financing German industry. The situation is gradually changing, largely as a result of global privatisations, for example Deutsche Telekom, and the coming to the market of many smaller firms, particularly on the Neuer Markt.

*Deutsche Börse*
In Germany, investors can buy and sell shares on any of eight stock

exchanges or on the electronic trading system Xetra. These collectively make up the Deutsche Börse, in which the Frankfurt Stock Exchange is dominant. Frankfurt accounts for about three-quarters of the total turnover in securities in Germany. Xetra, the electronic trading platform, was introduced in 1997. It has enabled Frankfurt to consolidate its dominant position in the German markets.

The eight stock exchanges and Xetra, and DTB, the futures and options exchange now merged into Eurex, all operate under the umbrella of a parent company, Deutsche Börse AG, that is also responsible for the settlement of all exchange transactions in securities and futures in Germany.

Each share that is listed in Germany is assigned to one of three market segments

- Official trading
- The second segment
- The third segment.

The Neuer Markt, a market specially established for rapid-growth companies, is an independent trading segment within the third segment. However, despite being classified in the third segment, Neuer Markt companies must meet the listing criteria for second segment companies, for example requirements for high standards of transparency and unconditional continuous trading of their shares.

Deutsche Börse also has developed an additional segment called SMAX that is designed to appeal to Mid Cap companies that lack the profile for the official trading list, but that wish to avoid becoming lost in the long lists of second or third segment companies.

*Trading, settlement and transfer*
Investors can have their orders executed either on the floor of one of the stock exchanges or through Xetra that now accounts for a large majority of trades in the shares of the top companies, the Dax 30 securities.

The settlement system is fully computerised. All securities traded in Frankfurt are held in a central depository, the Deutsche Kassenverein.

Transfer of ownership of shares is by simple book entry from the seller's to the buyer's account. At the same time, the Kassenverein debits or credits cash accounts held by the stock exchange members with the clearing house.

# France

The Paris exchange uses a computerised order-driven trading system called the CAC (the Compagnie Nationale des Agents de Change). This system also covers securities traded in the regional exchanges: these closed their trading floors in the late 1980s when a national stock market, the Paris Bourse, was created.

There are three markets within the French stock exchange

- The main market (Cote Officielle). This consists of a cash market (marché au comptant) where trades are settled for cash on T+3, and a monthly account market (marché à règlement mensuel) where trades are settled at the end of each month.
- The second market. This has been extended with the addition of a market for new high-technology and high-growth companies, the Nouveau Marché.
- A market for small companies, the Marché Hors-Cote. Companies listing on this market do not have to issue a prospectus and are subject to minimum disclosure requirements.

*Settlement and transfer*
French securities are identifiable bearer securities, dematerialised and held in electronic book entry form with authorised intermediaries (banks, stock exchange member firms, etc.). Each authorised intermediary has an account with the central depository authority, Sicovam that is responsible for settling all trades on the Paris Bourse.

The clearing and settlement system in use is called Relit. Under Relit, orders are matched automatically in the CAC trading system, and trades need no further confirmation. Automatic delivery and payment take place simultaneously on T+3, i.e. there is a delivery versus payment system in operation.

In 1999, the Paris Bourse and Sicovam signed a memorandum of understanding to set up a joint European Clearing House (ECH) in a joint venture with Cédel International and Deutsche Börse Clearing.

# Italy

The regulatory structure of the Italian stock market was radically altered by a legislative decree in 1996. In 1997 the Italian Stock Exchange Council set up a new private company, Borsa Italiana, that is now responsible for the regulation, promotion and management of the Stock Exchange, the Unlisted Securities Market and the Italian Derivatives Market (IDEM).

The Italian stock market is based in Milan. It has four main equity trading sections

- The main market, now supplemented by the Nuevo Mercato (similar in concept to the Neuer Markt and the Nouveau Marché)
- The Unlisted Securities Market (Mercato Ristretto)
- The odd lot market that can be accessed only by market professionals
- IDEM, the Italian derivatives market.

The main market uses a screen-based, electronic order-driven trading system, and settlement is on T+5.

# Spain

In Spain, the Securities Market Act recognises the following official secondary markets

- Stock exchanges
- The public debt market, organised by the Bank of Spain
- Futures and options markets.

The Economics and Finance ministry is empowered to authorise the creation of more official markets. Valencia's citric fruits futures market was recognised as an official market in 1995.

The stock exchanges in Spain (Madrid, Bilbao, Barcelona and Valencia) are the official secondary markets for trading shares. Companies also use the stock markets for primary issues to raise finance. Fixed income securities, both government and corporate debt securities, also are traded via the stock markets.

The main stock exchange is in Madrid (Bolsa de Madrid). It uses two trading systems, an open outcry system that has now virtually disappeared, and an electronic order-driven trading system, SIBE. All four stock exchanges have a stake in SIBE.

The settlement and clearing of securities traded on the stock exchanges, except for government debt securities, is handled by the SCLV (Servicio de Compensación Liquidación de Valores). The SCLV is responsible for recording the securities that are represented in book entry form, whether they are traded or not. In other words, the SCLV acts as a central registry for the book entry system.

# Euro.NM and the European small cap markets

*Euro.NM*
Euro.NM is a pan-European stock market comprising five members, the

stock markets of Amsterdam, Brussels, Germany, France and Italy. Euro.NM specialises in high-growth companies, i.e. those listed on the relevant high-growth stock markets in the member countries (the Neuer Markt, Nouveau Marché, etc.).

The individual stock markets within the Euro.NM consortium observe common rules and standards. The national markets work together to promote jointly listed companies and to provide transparent access to any stock on any other exchange within the consortium.

This means for example that the Euro.NM network will provide investors access to shares traded on the Neuer Markt, the Nouveau Marché, and so on.


*Easdaq*

The Easdaq Stock Market is based in Brussels. It was established in 1996 and operates across 14 European countries with one rule book and one trading and settlement system. It is a European market for high-growth companies and is based on the Nasdaq model.

Europe has a large number of stock markets and a large number of different languages. With just one rule book, one trading system and one settlement system, Easdaq is able to offer a single transparent market to its investors, its members and its listed companies.

It is a screen-based, quote-driven market. It uses a multiple market-maker system, similar to the one used by Nasdaq.

On-screen quotations are provided by market makers. Prices are quoted in the currency chosen by the company at the time it applied for admission to listing, typically in euros but quite often in dollars. There are real-time information feeds of Easdaq prices to information vendors including Bloomberg and Reuters.

The Easdaq market is open from 09.30 to 16.30 Central European Time. Trade reporting and matching facilities are available outside these hours. Only registered market makers can enter price (and size) quotations for a security. A market maker must be willing to purchase and sell securities on its own account, on a continuous basis, during normal business hours. They must maintain continuous two-way prices in shares for which they are registered as market makers throughout this time.

Transactions, once made, are confirmed and settled using TRAX, a global communications network operated by the International Securities Market Association, ISMA. TRAX has a direct link to both Euroclear and Cedel, where the actual settlement of Easdaq market transactions takes place.

# Japan

A significant overhaul of the Japanese financial markets, a Japanese big bang took place in 1998. Reforms were implemented, aimed at promoting competition within the securities industry through deregulation. For example, restrictions on off-exchange trading for listed securities were abolished.

To reduce costs and improve operational efficiency, the Tokyo Stock Exchange closed its trading floor in 1999: until then, the 150 most actively traded Japanese stocks were traded on the floor of the exchange. Orders are now entered into the system from terminals in members' offices.

*First Section and Second Section securities*
Securities on the Tokyo Stock Exchange are in two sections:

- The first section (Alpha section) consists of the shares of the large listed companies. These make up most of the market capitalisation.
- The second section consists of newly quoted securities and unlisted securities that would otherwise have to be traded over the counter, outside the exchange.

All securities must be traded through authorised securities dealers who are members of the Japanese Securities Dealers Association. Most major foreign brokers are members.

All quoted shares in Japan are in registered form. Japan is unusual in that the transfer of shares does not require the signature of the seller. Transfer can be effected either by physical delivery of stock certificates or by means of a book entry transfer system, JASDAQ. Settlement is normally on T+3.

Securities companies, financial institutions and others open accounts with a depository bank and deposit their stocks with that bank. Subsequent securities transactions are cleared by a single entry in the books of these banks, rather than by an actual movement of share certificates.

Securities cannot be delivered outside Japan, and so safe custody facilities are obligatory for foreign investors in Japanese stocks.

In 1998, the Tokyo Stock Exchange decided to adopt a delivery versus payment system of settlement, setting a target date for implementation of March 2001.

From May 1999, the Tokyo Stock Exchange also has operated as a clearing house. It now acts as the central counterparty for all trades executed on the exchange, and it guarantees settlement for all such transactions.

The main legislation governing securities trading and securities listing is the Securities and Exchange Law. The Ministry of Finance also plays an active role in governing the markets and approving new share issues.

# Hong Kong

The Stock Exchange of Hong Kong was incorporated in 1980 as a result of a merger of four stock exchanges. Computerised trading on the unified exchange began in 1986.

The exchange trades shares in Hong Kong companies as well as H shares, i.e. shares in mainland Chinese companies.

The exchange's trading system is electronic, and allows for trading in shares both on and off the floor of the exchange. Further system enhancements will make it possible for a trading interface between investors, their brokers and the exchange, enabling investors to have direct access to the exchange trading system.

Trading on the Hong Kong Exchange, as in Tokyo, is on a board lot system. Lot sizes vary according to the price of the shares.

Brokers sit at terminals into which they enter details of orders. Transactions are then usually agreed by telephone. Conversations are recorded automatically, and recordings provide evidence of the contract price, size and direction, i.e. who is buying and who is selling.

Transactions are settled on T+, between dealers' offices. There is no central settlement facility within the exchange, nor is there a centralised book entry system. Shares are in registered form.

# Emerging Markets

*Features of an emerging market*
Emerging markets is a catch-all term to describe markets outside North America, mature Europe, Japan, Hong Kong and the Anglo-Saxon Asian economies of Australia and New Zealand.

However, an emerging market normally will have some of the following generic features

- A national economy with a low-to-middling gross domestic product
- A national economy with a low gross domestic product per head of population

- Unreliable national economic statistics
- An extensive black economy
- A fast pace of technological change
- Restricted information on companies.

The companies in major emerging markets tend to have several common features. Unless they have come to the market as a result of a government privatisation, companies tend to have the following characteristics

- Closely controlled by a small number of shareholders
- Dominated by the company's founding members and their heirs
- Majority of shares are held by family members
- A public listing was made originally for reasons other than raising capital, for example to avoid tax
- Extensive cross-shareholdings between companies.

There are probably around 100 country stock markets to which the term emerging market could be ascribed. Emerging market stock exchanges need not use out-of-date technology for their trading systems: an exchange can buy in the technology from a more developed market.

An emerging market stock market is likely to have some of the following features

- Small total market capitalisation of companies when compared to more advanced markets
- Modest or low trading volumes
- More volatile share prices than in developed markets
- Poor or unenforced regulatory structure
- Only a basic market infrastructure (market professionals, etc)
- An unclear legal system
- Listing rules and trading procedures that differ substantially from accepted western practises
- Poor financial disclosure
- Different classes and prices of shares for foreign investors
- Only loose adherence to accounting standards by listed companies

- Inefficient settlement and clearing systems
- Inefficient custody systems.

*Reasons for investing in emerging markets*

In recent years, emerging markets have on the whole been a poor investment, particularly in comparison to the returns available in more developed markets. This situation may change.

The basic principle behind a decision to invest in emerging markets is that higher returns should be available as a reward for the higher investment risk. However, this has not in general proved to be the case.

Emerging markets remain a long-term investment, and it remains to be seen whether long-term returns will justify the extra risk of investing capital in markets with under-developed infrastructures.

In principle, the reasons for investing in emerging markets would be

- Emerging markets should develop at a faster rate than more developed economies.
- Domestic consumer markets in emerging markets should expand rapidly, as life expectancy rises and standards of living improve.
- Securities are valued on lower earnings or EBITDA multiples, or on a lower market value: asset value ratio, than securities in developed markets.
- Privatisations of government-owned industries should offer opportunities for foreign investors to acquire attractive stock at a reasonable price.

# Glossary

**American option**
This option can be exercised at any time up to and including its expiry date.

**At the money**
This is when the strike price is the same as the current exchange rate. At the money spot (ATMS) is a strike price equal to the current spot rate. At-the-money forward (ATMF) is a strike price equal to the current forward exchange rate for the same exercise/maturity date. An option is said to be at the money when it is ATMS and a European option is at the money when it is ATMF.

**Currency future**
These are a special form of exchange-traded forward contract, for standard quantities of currency and a settlement date fixed by the futures exchange. The main currency futures exchange is the Chicago Mercantile Exchange (CME) in Chicago. A buyer of a currency future contracts to buy one currency in exchange for another (usually dollars). A seller of a currency future contracts to sell one currency in exchange for another (usually dollars).

**Currency risk**
Currency risk arises from the potential consequences of an adverse movement in foreign exchange rates. It consists of transaction, translation and economic exposures.

**Currency swap**
This is an agreement between two parties for an exchange of payments.

One party makes payments in one currency and the counterparty makes payments in a second currency.

### Currency option

A currency option gives its holder the right *without the obligation* either to buy (call option) or sell (put option) a quantity of currency at a future date, at an agreed rate of exchange. The amount of currency that is bought or sold is specified in the option agreement. A European option can be exercised only on its specified expiry date. An American option can be exercised at any time up to and including its expiry date.

### Direct economic exposures

These arise from expected but as yet uncommitted future receipts or payments in foreign currency.

### Economic exposures

These arise when the trading position of a business is at risk to adverse movements in exchange rates. These exposures can be either short or long term, direct or indirect.

### European option

This type of option can be exercised only on a specified expiry date.

### Exercising an option

This is when the holder of an option takes up the right to buy or sell currency under the terms of the option.

### Factoring

This is a way for companies to outsource the collecting of debts. For example, a factor can collect money due to an exporter's customers, and pass on receipts (less fees, etc) to the exporter. A factor also will lend against the security of invoiced and unpaid export debts.

### Forward contract

This is a commitment between a customer and a bank to trade, at some specified future date, a quantity of one exchange for another, at an agreed (fixed) rate of exchange. They are used to fix an exchange rate now for a future transaction, eliminating the currency exposure. The settlement date can be arranged to suit the customer's requirement. (See value-date option contract.)

## Hedging

Hedging action might be taken to avoid, reduce or eliminate a currency exposure. Risk-averse companies will hedge exposures. Companies are more likely to hedge short-term transaction exposures than less certain and longer-term direct economic exposures.

## Indirect economic exposures

These are long-term risks based on exchange rate movements over time benefiting foreign competitors by giving them a cost or price advantage in world markets.

## In the money

This is when the strike price of an option is more favorable to the option holder than the current spot market exchange rate (American option) or the forward exchange rate for the same exercise/expiry date (European option). If an option is in the money at expiry, it will be exercised unless in the case of an American option, it has been exercised earlier.

## Offset hedging or transaction-based structural hedging

This is the matching of transactions such as receipts and spending in the same currency. Receipts also can be matched with payments for currencies in the same currency bloc, normally without significant risk.

## Out of the money

This is when the strike price is less favorable to the option holder than the current market rate of exchange (American option) or the forward rate for the same expiry/maturity date (European options). If an option is out of the money on its expiry date, it will not be exercised.

## Purchasing Power Parity (PPP) Theory

This theory predicts that in the long term, the rate of exchange between two currencies will alter in accordance with the relative rate of price inflation between the countries concerned.

## Strike price

This is the rate of exchange at which the currency can be bought or sold. This is specified in the option agreement. It could be the same as the current market rate (at the money), more favorable (in the money) or less favorable (out of the money).

## Structural hedging

This reduces currency risk by matching revenue and payments, or assets or liabilities, in each currency. Foreign currency bank accounts simplify structural hedging.

## Tender-to-contract (TTC) cover

This can be obtained as a hedge for this currency risk, either from banks or from the Export Credit Guarantee Department in the UK. For TTC cover, the company pays a premium in return for fixing the exchange rate for the foreign currency income from the contract, in the event that the contract is won. It also can be arranged as a currency option.

## Transaction exposure

Arises with a commitment to make a payment or receive income in a foreign currency at a future date. There is a risk that an adverse exchange rate movement before the payment or receipt occurs could increase costs or reduce income in the domestic currency.

## Translation exposure

Arises for parent companies with foreign subsidiaries. There is a risk of reporting lower profits or exchange losses in the consolidated accounts of the group because of exchange rate movements.

**Value-date option contract**

This is when a forward contract is arranged for settlement at any time between two specified dates.

# Index

# Notes

# Notes

# Notes

# Notes

# Notes

# Notes

# Notes

# Notes

# Notes

# Notes